THE CITY

IN

THE WORLD

OF

THE FUTURE

THE

CITY
IN
THE WORLD
OF
THE FUTURE

BY

HAL HELLMAN

PUBLISHED BY

M. Evans and Company, Inc. NEW YORK

AND DISTRIBUTED IN ASSOCIATION WITH

J. B. Lippincott Company

PHILADELPHIA AND NEW YORK

FOR JENNIFER

who will live in a city of the future

The author wishes to thank Mr. Crawford C. Westbrook, Director of Planning, Gruen Associates, who both provided material and reviewed the manuscript.

H.H.

Contents

Prologue

ANDREW MANN AND his family had spent the day in Recreation Zone 14, outside City Dome 2. It had been a lovely day. The sun felt good; and while the air inside the city's domes was always fresh and clear, it somehow never had the pungence of a crisp autumn day on the outside.

They had hiked, and picnicked, and fished in the stream, but now it was time to go. Andrew had radioed for a heli-bus, and they were waiting for it at one of the outlying stations. It was expected in ten minutes. But a brisk wind had sprung up, and the sky was rapidly filling with dark, menacing clouds. Darn it, Andrew thought, I keep forgetting about these changes in the weather on the outside.

Just then, a warning buzzer sounded and an insta-shelter erected itself around them. And just in time too, for the first big drops were starting to fall. Moments later, the storm burst in all its fury.

Nevertheless the small, unpiloted heli-bus arrived on time. It swooped down and landed on the grass right next to the shelter. Janis, Andrew's teenage daughter, and her younger brother Jimmy climbed into the two front seats, while Andrew and Mrs. Mann sat in the rear. Andrew snapped the door shut and the heli-bus rose straight up into the air.

As they sped back toward Dome 4, which enclosed their section of the city, Jimmy asked, "Dad, how does the heli-bus know where to go?"

"Well, when I radioed Transportation Central, I told them where we were and where we wanted to go. They simply programmed the automatic flight control system to home-in on the station where we were waiting, and then to take us to Domeport 4."

"Oh," said Jimmy. "It's as simple as that. Hm."

Andrew noticed that the weather was already beginning to clear. He was glad, for a view from the air was the only way to take in the incredible size of Eastern Region 1, which stretched from oldtime Boston in the north to Richmond, Virginia, in the south. It would be an impressive sight to anyone; but it was especially so to him for he had been brought up in the hinterlands, where a region of 75 million was thought to be big. Eastern Region 2, of course, started just below "1" and continued down to the lower tip of Florida.

What he liked about New Boston, their home, was the city's logical organization and structure. Consisting of two intersecting "linear cities," each in turn comprised of six domes lying in a line, the city's organization and X-shaped structure were quite clear, at least from the air.

He wondered how long the open space and recreation areas between the arms of the city would remain open, for the country's population was still increasing rapidly. Even now the city computers were debating whether to add domes to the ends of the arms, or to begin new arms.

He wondered too who had first thought of crossing two linear cities. All the domes were now interconnected by high speed tube transit; this cut down considerably on the air congestion which had begun to reach disastrous proportions. The whole idea had worked out very well and was being copied elsewhere.

They were passing over Dome 1. This was the first part of New Boston to be domed over, and so it was still covered in glastic—a slightly old-fashioned but still serviceable combination of glass and plastic. The glastic domes were the first ones that were able to capture the sun's heat in the summer and convert it to power. As with each of the city's domes, Dome 1 had a heliport at its summit.

As the heli-bus dropped softly onto Domeport 4, Andrew's eye was caught by the spidery pattern of the rideways radiating out from the domeport to the twenty or so buildings that were tall enough to intersect the dome. Thanks to the transportation grid contained within the dome—and which, being almost a mile up in the air, was quite invisible from the ground!—pressure on the ground transportation system was eased and a completely new route for travel within Dome 4 was created.

They changed to the ele-car marked "District 14," which carried them swiftly along the gently curving, transparent rideway to Tower North. The ele-car stopped briefly in the sky lobby to pick up a waiting passenger, and then took them down to their apartment on the 152nd floor. While Mrs. Mann ordered dinner from the building's Central Service Department, Andrew checked the communications console for messages. There was one reminding Andrew and Jimmy that they had orchestra practice in the school auditorium (5th floor) at 20:30, and another reminding Janis that she had a tennis lesson on Recreation Terrace 1 (207th floor, north) at 20:00.

Mrs. Mann thought she might take a swim (208th floor) while Janis had her lesson.

Although the apartment was not the best one they ever had —for example it lacked the latest in RHM (Robot Home

5

Maintenance)—it was convenient to Andrew's firm, which had its offices on the 33rd floor of the tower.

From their dining balcony, they looked out over the city and even beyond, to the bay. There they could see the first of the seven neighborhoods that were eventually to comprise Floating City now taking shape in the shipyard. After this first neighborhood was completed it would be floated to its mooring and anchored alongside Dome 4 to take some of the pressure off the housing and office shortage. Because of the monolithic (single-structure) design of the neighborhood, a weather-control dome was not necessary. As the other neighborhoods were built, they would be added to the first, until the whole had become a full-fledged floating city. At that point a "city center" platform, containing theaters, specialty shops, a medical center, and the like would be added.

Now that considerable experience had been gained in the building of floating cities, it had been suggested that the idea of a seagoing city should be considered. Clearly the bulky, pyramidal design of the neighborhood was not a good one for ocean travel; but building a more streamlined, powered city of ten or twenty thousand inhabitants was no problem. The question was, were enough people interested in living on such a "ship city" to make the idea practicable. Andrew, who had been working at his present position for five years and was entitled to a year off with pay, thought he might be interested. Others, like artists and writers, might be able to take their work with them. And, with the ready availability of three-dimensional visual communications, even executives and others might be able to operate quite successfully from a floating city.

A market survey was being taken by the shipbuilding con-

6

cern to test the idea. "Perhaps," thought Andrew, "a leisurely world cruise would be fun."

Andrew explained the idea to the family. They were intrigued; Mrs. Mann said, "It sounds like a lovely idea, but what about the children's education?"

"No problem," said Andrew. "There would be full education facilities through high school on board. Remember, this would be a city, not a ship."

1

What Is A City?

BY THE TIME the 21st century arrives, it is expected that the population of the United States will have soared from the present 200 million to 300 million and perhaps even higher.

This is equivalent to saying that we will have to build four hundred more cities of a quarter of a million inhabitants each! And this does not include rebuilding existing housing that will continue to deteriorate as the years go by. For example, 62 per cent of the housing in Pittsburgh is already over forty-five years old.

Of course, we could also build twenty cities of 5 million each, or four thousand cities of 25,000 each. Any way you figure it, that's a lot of building. Alternatively, we could try somehow to squeeze all these additional people into existing cities.

But the main point is that most of them *will* live in and around cities. Even today, in spite of our farm and frontier heritage, almost 75 per cent of all Americans live in urban areas.

And if present population trends continue (see chart) the percentage will increase, as it has increased in the past quarter century. It has been predicted that by the end of the century 90–95 per cent of all Americans will live in urban areas. The

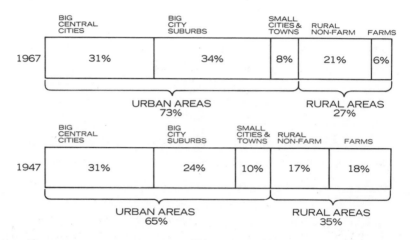

WHERE AMERICANS LIVE

implications of all this are staggering. One estimate has it that between now and the year 2000 as much urban building will be carried out as in all man's history to date.

The chart shows something else of interest. Central cities have not increased in population at all. Even the number of persons visiting big city centers has tended to remain about the same.

The big growth has been, and probably will continue to be, in the suburbs of these big cities. But this kind of growth creates serious problems, which are expressed in such terms as suburban sprawl and Spread City, U.S.A. Another term that is sometimes used is "slurb." Although actually a con-

10

traction for slum suburb, a slurb has also been described as
a suburban sprawl tied to an urban mess by a confusion of
roads.

Suburbs, with a lower density of population, cannot efficiently provide public transit, schools, and services. People
may move to the surburbs but they want city conveniences.
For example, in the suburbs the only way to get around efficiently is by car. But the poor cannot afford cars, and so
cannot conveniently get to jobs and entertainment. Further,
cars produce noxious gases and, equally troublesome, they
need roads, roads, roads. In Los Angeles, perhaps two-thirds
of the land has been given over to roads, interchanges, and
parking areas.

Those who have moved to the "country" for some peace
and quiet, and to escape the high costs of city living, begin

*A major highway interchange in Florida uses
up an enormous amount of land.*

to find that life in the suburbs is not quite as idyllic as they were led to believe it would be. Open land disappears under houses, industry and shopping centers, and taxes skyrocket to support the building of schools, sewers, and other services needed in new areas.

As suburban growth continues, another effect is seen. The suburbs of neighboring cities and towns begin to run into each other, making a solid, congealed mass of houses, roads, factories, and gas stations. For instance, New York City grew, on paper, from 2.5 million residents in 1891 to 7.9 million in 1950. In truth, it began to merge with such nearby cities as Jersey City and Newark, New Jersey, and Stamford, Connecticut. The result has been a metropolitan area that now includes some 20 million inhabitants.

This, then, is the metropolis (from the Greek *mētēr*, mother, and *polis*, city) that you have been hearing so much about— a large collection of cities, towns, and suburbs with a central city that provides much of the employment and entertainment for the others. With the help of modern transportation, the metropolis has attained a commuting radius of fifty or more miles from the center, permitting it to grow more than a hundred times larger than the largest cities of the past. It is in these outlying areas that the major population growth is taking place.

The City—Pro and Con

I should point out that metropolitan growth is *not* happening because there is no more room left elsewhere. The United States is a big country, with more than 3 million square miles of land area. This works out to an average of 66 persons per square mile. As a point of comparison, we note that the population density of New York City averages out to some 25,000 inhabitants per square mile. Further, the area of Manhattan south of Central Park comprises only nine square miles. Yet in addition to its own residents, some 3 million additional people enter the area every working day.

Clearly, the United States is a long way from "Standing Room Only," even if we discount uninhabitable areas like mountain tops and canyon bottoms. However, with modern heating, transportation, and construction techniques, there are not many places where man cannot live. Indeed, such areas can encourage the most challenging and startling kinds of architecture. Snow-filled places like Vail and Snowmass-at-Aspen, both in Colorado, are examples of attractive, planned vacation communities that are springing up across the country in the most unlikely places.

In any case, the point to be made is that fully 70 per cent of all Americans live on only about 2 per cent of the land! So if they are crowded, we know whose fault that is. And, again, the trend is continuing in that direction. What will happen, you may ask, when metropolises begin to grow together? This too is already happening, and has been given a name: *megalopolis.** It is expected that someday the majority of Americans will be living in only three such areas: one, stretching from the Boston area down to Washington, D.C.; a second in the Great Lakes region; and the third along the Pacific Coast, from San Francisco down to San Diego. A fourth, on a smaller scale, may develop in the

* The term "conurbation" is also sometimes used to denote the same phenomenon.

southern part of Florida. The megalopolis is a large-scale concept, and can include many states.

The term derives from the two Greek words *megalo*, large or great, and *polis*, city. It is interesting to note that the name was originally given by the ancient Greeks to a town which they hoped would become the largest in Greece. But it remained a small town. As someone once said: "A small town is a big city that never made it."

Nevertheless, 16 million Americans live in small towns.

And if rural areas, both farm and non-farm are included, another 54 million Americans are included. Clearly the non-big-city way of life also has something to offer.

As a matter of fact those who think about this kind of thing—town and city planners, architects, politicians, sociologists—seem to fall into two major camps: the city lovers and the city haters.

The city haters blame all the ills of society on the big city. It is said to be the cause of violence, drug addiction, mental illness, crime, nervousness, broken families, and whatever else is bad. The great architect Frank Lloyd Wright referred to city dwellers as "herd-struck morons our present sky-scraperism has cultivated," and as "human beings, all crawling on hard pavements like ants to hole in somewhere or find their way to this or that cubicle."

Somewhat less violent was Ralph Waldo Emerson's comment: "Cities force growth and make men talkative and entertaining, but they make them artificial." His point is clear: country people are "real" (whatever that may mean); city people are false and artificial.

Genghis Khan, the brilliant thirteenth-century Mongol leader, felt so threatened by cities that he completely wiped out a number of them in his sweep across Asia.

14

Wright divided the primitive human race into two classes: the cave dweller and the nomad or wanderer. Note how subtly he draws his case against the cave dweller, which he equated with the present-day city person.

We assume the cave-dweller multiplied with comparative ease owing to this safety [i.e. the safety provided by the cave], and more rapidly than his brother the wanderer. But when his defenses fell, destruction was more complete, economic waste more terrific. So when he ceased to find a natural cave, he learned to make one. . . . The cave-dweller's nomadic human counterpart meantime cultivated mobility for safety. Defenses, for him, lay in the idea—or swiftness, stratagem, and such arts of self-defense as nature taught.

I imagine the ideal of freedom which keeps breaking through our present static establishments [cities] . . . is due in no small degree to survival of the original instincts of the nomad—the adventurer: he who kept his freedom by his undivided prowess beneath the stars rather than he who lived by his obedience and labor in the deep shadow of the wall.

Wright's approach in city planning is summed up in his words: "Man is returning to the descendants of the wandering tribe—the adventurers, I hope."

But, as we mentioned earlier, they are not. They are swarming to the cities in ever increasing numbers. The city lovers would point out that no one is forcing them into these "vast prisons with glass fronts" and that the great majority of the inhabitants have come willingly—often joyously—to escape the dullness, drabness, and lack of stimulation and opportunity of many rural areas.

The city lovers would add that this is by no means all to the bad. The ingestion of great numbers of different kinds of people may give the big city indigestion or even worse

15

once in a while, but these immigrants, with their strange habits and ways, are what make the cities interesting, diverse, and exciting. The philosopher Paul Tillich wrote: "By its nature, the metropolis provides what otherwise could be given only by travel; namely, the strange." In some large cities, practically every nationality in the world is represented.

And where else but in a city the size of New York can you find so many different specialty high schools: the High School of Music and Art, Bronx High School of Science, Fashion Institute of Technology, Food and Maritime Trades Vocational High School, New York School of Printing, High School of Art and Design, Automotive High School, and many others—including a high school that gives a major in agriculture!

The French architect Le Corbusier had this to say about Paris: "What moves me in Paris is its vitality. She has been living on her present site now for more than a thousand years, always beautiful and always lauded, always new and always being renewed. . . . Paris is alive!"

It is not the object of this book to mediate between the city lovers and the city haters. Rather it is to emphasize that not only does man build cities, but that cities also build man. The Finnish-American architect Eliel Saarinen expressed it this way: ". . . man's physical and mental development depend largely upon the character of the environment in which he is nurtured as a child, where he spends his manhood, and where he does his work."

But town and city planning may take a generation or more —several tens of years—to come to fruition. So we must plan now for the years ahead.

The first step is to look at what is possible.

16

2

New Building Techniques

A SMALL TRUCK drives into an empty lot. Two men get out. They do some preliminary work, which includes unlimbering a special boom carried on the back of the truck. Then they punch some buttons and set some dials and the boom literally begins to "spin" a house—in a manner not very different from the way a spider spins his web, except that the boom spins solid wall as it goes along.

The key to the technique is the erector boom and the traveling mold at the end of it. As the mold travels along, guided by a small computer in the truck, a foaming plastic is pushed out (extruded) and begins to both expand and harden within ten seconds. Two steel plates guide the material into place as shown in the drawing, and cause the outer skin of the material to become hard and dense, while the inner mass remains fluffy and air filled. The result is a solid, but light, material with excellent insulating properties.

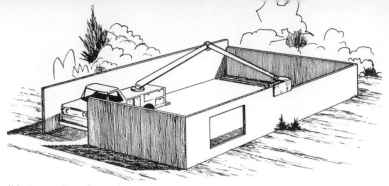

"Spinning" a house.

Six or seven hours later the job is finished. A house, complete with walls, ceiling and interior partitions, stands on the site. Neither the inside nor the outside needs paint or other covering, for the finish is automatically created—it can be plain, patterned, and/or colored as desired. Cost so far of a 25 by 40 foot house: $3,800.

Farfetched? Not at all. The technique has already been laid out and a prototype of the traveling mold is being built. Developed by a group consisting of an architect and several university scientists, the technique can be used for any shape—square, rectangular, circular or eliptical, and for any type of structure—houses, factories, warehouses, perhaps even highrise structures.

While no structure has actually been made in this manner, it will be done. And, as we shall shortly see, a number of other new construction techniques have been developed and tried out.

Yet, in an age when man is traveling to the moon, exploring the ocean floor, and extracting energy from atoms, he still builds virtually all his houses in the same way he has been doing it for centuries. In general, he still digs a hole in the ground, lays a foundation, erects a frame of wood and covers the whole thing with strips or chunks of some material or other.

18

But why dig a hole and pour or build a foundation? Chemicals have been developed that can harden or solidify the earth in a short time. For single family houses, this would be quite adequate.

And while vast and increasing numbers of people are in dire need of decent housing, the builder still drives something like 70,000 nails by hand into 30,000 different pieces for most private houses he builds. In an age when rocket shells are automatically "spun" from fiber glass thread, he still builds houses by erecting four walls and putting a roof over them.

Even the ways of building the metal frames for his larger commercial buildings have not changed in a hundred years. Each girder is hoisted by a crane, swung into place, and bolted or welded to the frame. Bridges too are normally built this way. But when the Verrazano Narrows Bridge, one of the newest and most magnificent in the world, was put up, giant sections were "factory built," floated down the river in barges, and then swung into place by giant cranes.

The advantages to this method are several. First, the weather is a major problem in construction work. With this technique a large part of the work can be done indoors, which makes at least that part of the work independent of rain, snow, and ice.

Secondly, work inside a properly designed building can be far more efficient, with proper tools, machines, handling devices, and special jigs and fixtures readily available. Also, because these are available, the designer is more likely to try to design a number of identical pieces, which makes for economy in building.

Prefabrication

The idea of prefabricated houses immediately springs to mind, i.e., vast numbers of cheap, mass-produced, identical houses standing next to each other. Probably the best known of these were the small houses built shortly after World War II in what is now Levittown, Long Island.

These little houses have been severely criticized by architectural critics, by sociologists, by psychologists, and by a number of other high-class professionals who didn't have to live in them—in other words, by those who could afford better.

But for many thousands who might have otherwise been stuck in two-room basement apartments in a slum neighborhood, these houses—which could be bought or rented for a very low figure, considering the shortage of housing at the time—provided very adequate housing. I have spoken to a number of early inhabitants who have since moved on. Without exception, they looked back with satisfaction on their years there.

Actually, there are various levels of prefabrication, of which the most basic is the manufacture of precut parts in large numbers. These are then assembled into "bundles" and delivered to the various sites, where they are erected by a builder. This is how the Levittown houses were put up, and the method is widely used in the United States today.

Another type utilizes the idea of "panelization": the preparation of various sizes and kinds of interior and exterior wall panels which can be fitted together in different arrangements. Many office buildings are now built in this manner, using

20

Prebuilt wall and ceiling panels lock into place and speed up construction.

what is called "curtain-wall" construction. That is, the walls do not support anything, but are hung on the steel frame. A large number of lower, warehouse-type buildings are also being built in this way. The builders claim advantages in cost, and building times of weeks rather than months or years. They claim too that the buildings, being pre-engineered, are better engineered.

Home builders and home owners are also reaping benefits from panelization, a common use being the interior wood paneling which is being used in vast amounts throughout the country. Whereas a carpenter's skill used to be necessary to cut and install the separate strips of wood paneling, today the large (e.g. 4 foot by 8 foot) sheets can be rapidly and easily installed by almost anyone, often with glue or clips. A wide variety of textures and colors are available.

It should be noted that these forms of prefabrication are by no means new. Although they only became popular after World War II, to help make up for the many needed build-

*The Crystal Palace, an early and spectacular
example of prefabrication.*

ings that were *not* built during the war, the techniques actually go back much further. One of the very first, and surely
one of the most spectacular, examples is that of the Crystal
Palace. This 1,851-foot building (one-third of a mile), contained an area of almost twenty-one acres, yet was put together in only six months for the first International World's
Fair Exposition (1851) in Hyde Park, London. The "secret"
that made this possible was the prefabrication of small glass,
iron, and wood pieces. (Most of the pieces were relatively
small because the largest glass panels that could be manufactured at the time were only four feet wide.) All the parts
were carefully preplanned, manufactured in various shops,
delivered to the site and bolted together. An interesting dem-
onstration of the capabilities of such construction was given
when the entire building was dismantled three years later and
reconstructed elsewhere! The new location was Syndenham;
there the great building remained as a museum and concert

22

hall until 1936 when it was damaged by fire. It was finally torn down in 1941 because it provided too good a target for enemy bombers during World War II.

Modularization

There is yet another step in the prefabrication of buildings, one that comes closer to the example of the Verrazano Narrows Bridge. Here various parts of a house or office building (e.g. a wall, a whole room, or even several rooms) are factory built, hauled to the site and installed in various ways. The process is called modularization, and is based on the idea of a module, which is a mass-produced unit of housing or other

The world's first "flying hotel room"?

construction. Now we begin to really see the potentialities of new technology.

In San Antonio, Texas, a twenty-one-story hotel, the Palacio del Rio, was put up in 202 days, less than half the time conventional construction would have taken. Each room of the hotel was cast in concrete (like a hollow box with a cover) in a plant several miles from the hotel site. The inside of the box was completely painted, carpeted and furnished—right down to light bulbs and ash trays—before it was hauled to the site. Just 127 days after ground-breaking the first of the five hundred rooms was lifted into place by a specially built crane. More than two thousand people were on hand to see what was undoubtedly the world's first flying hotel room.

This description is more real than literary, for the flat wall surfaces put the units at the mercy of even the smallest puffs of wind. As a result, the engineers had to rig each unit with a stabilizing device similar to that used on a helicopter!

In a variation of the concrete box method, Michigan State University is planning a health-care center which would involve the erection of a central core. Then prefinished laboratories and other rooms would be hoisted into place and simply "plugged" into the central tower. It is estimated that apartments could be built at a savings of 18 per cent over conventional methods—if a large enough market, about one thousand modules a year, could be found.

This really is the heart of the situation. The initial investment in equipment is very high, and one can never be sure that enough additional units will be sold to cover this early investment.

Another idea is to bring the factory to the site. This eliminates the problem of hauling large units from place to place.

***Model of proposed Michigan State University
Health Care Center shows how modules can be
"plugged" into central tower.***

In planning the construction process, a balance must be struck.
On the one hand, the larger the unit the more efficient the
process. But it is just as clear that the larger the unit, the
greater the problem of moving it.

One possible technique is shown on page 26. This ski lodge
and 300-seat restaurant was prebuilt in five sections, including
all furnishings and 10-foot picture windows. The sections were

25

airlifted one by one to the top of a 1,300-foot mountain, and set precisely on cinder block foundations. Naturally, concrete was not used to construct the units, for they would have been far too heavy for airlifting.

The builders estimated that doing the job this way saved about 20 per cent of the cost and 60 per cent of the time normally required. They added that if conventional methods had been required, the lodge might never have been placed on the summit of the mountain at all because of the difficult terrain.

Four of the sections measured 12 by 10 feet high, and two of them weighed about seven tons each. These large units necessitated the use of the giant Skycrane helicopter, one of

A Sikorsky Skycrane helicopter prepares to deposit the fourth of five units that will eventually be a ski-lodge and restaurant.

the largest in the world. Improvements in materials, however, may lessen the hauling problem. For example, the prefabricated plastic houses shown here weigh only 5,500 pounds and are easily deliverable by helicopter.

A lightweight concrete, called cellular concrete, has also been developed. A chemical substance "injected" into the concrete while it is being mixed causes tiny air bubbles to form. The resulting material is both light and strong, and retains its heat insulating properties as well, for dead air spaces are excellent insulators.

Concrete, it should be pointed out, is considered one of the great building materials. It has strength and, when properly used, provides great flexibility and attractiveness. The roof of the Kresge Auditorium at M.I.T., for example, is thinner in proportion to its size than the shell of an egg.

Prestressed concrete, a favorite building material for large structures, is formed by molding the concrete around steel bars or cables which have been put under stresses opposite to those they will sustain while in service. Then, when the normal loads are added, the concrete is in an essentially unstressed condition and holds up better.

Prefabricated plastic house designed by Matti Suuronen of Finland can be delivered by helicopter.

Other Materials, Other Approaches

At what might be called the opposite end of the pole we see the possibilities of inflatable shelters. These can be held in shape after inflation by keeping the' air pressure inside the enclosure higher than that outside by means of an air compressor. The structure simply remains blown up. Flimsy as the material may seem (it can be a rubberized fabric or thin, flexible plastic sheet), it is really quite tough. Also, being flexible, it gives with any kind of blow and does not tear easily. If it does it is easily patched.

Alternatively, the material may be such that it hardens after inflation, perhaps by the ultraviolet rays from the sun. If made thick enough and designed properly, the structure can be quite strong. An idea for a moon structure is shown here. The walls of the Stay Time Extension Module are two inches thick.

Yet another approach is to use the inflated structure as a kind of form, over which plastic foam or even concrete is sprayed, thus making a permanent structure.

Navy scientists are interested in the technique to help them overcome the problem of transporting bulky structures to out of the way places. The Upjohn Company has designed a "Geo-Hut" to house two men and their instruments. Since the "balloon" is only used as a form, it can be quite thin; indeed a two-man shelter needs only a pocket size balloon. The covering material foams when applied; thus relatively little of it is needed as well. The only bulky items needed are prefabricated window and door frames, vents, etc. These and any electrical wiring are laid against the balloon, after which a special air gun shoots a two-inch-thick layer of foam over the outside of the hut. As it hardens the foam expands to several

28

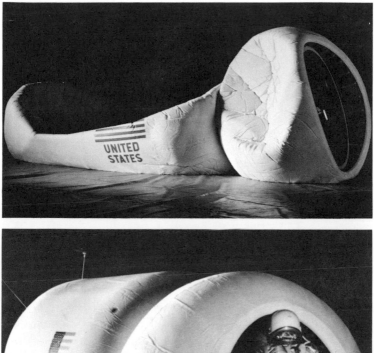

Prototype of the Stay Time Extension Module,
an expandable lunar shelter.

times its original thickness, and locks the frames, vents and wiring into place. The balloon can then be deflated, leaving a strong, snug, fireproof and chemically resistant "igloo" 9½ feet in diameter by 9½ feet high.

In the future it may not even be necessary to erect a form (e.g., the rubber balloon) first. It may be possible to make materials expand in only one or two directions, in which case walls and other broad surfaces could be "grown." By choosing the proper chemicals, plus careful planning and timing by computer, it is possible that the various constituents can successively form floors, walls and even ceilings. In other words, a house could be "grown" just as a tree or an animal grows into a predetermined form without outside interference.

The best-known plastic building ever put up was the House of Tomorrow at Disneyland in California. In the ten years of its existence, more than 20 million people saw it, not to speak of the millions more who admired the house in photographs. In all that time, the plastic walls showed no noticeable wear.

As a matter of fact the durability and strength of the house were demonstrated less while it was up, than when the wreckers wanted to tear it down. Normally the wrecker's iron ball can knock down a house of this size in no time at all. But the ball simply bounced off the walls. The job ended up taking two weeks instead of less than a day. They finally had to crush the house with specially designed "choker" cables.

Some materials, such as steel and other metals, are stronger in tension than in compression. That is, it takes far more force to pull a beam apart than to buckle it. The best visual evidence we have of this are the thin cables that support the decks of most of our large suspension bridges. For the future we can envision entire cities hung by slim cables from tall

30

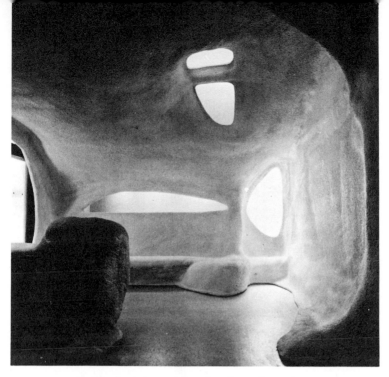

Sprayed environment of polyurethane foam.

central masts. The American architect/engineer/inventor R. Buckminster Fuller suggests that this might be a way to re-settle such places as New York's Harlem, for the buildings could be erected before the worst areas are demolished. Perhaps the ground level could even be left open for recreation purposes.

Research in new materials has given promise of far greater strengths than we are now used to. Materials called composites, which utilize the stiffness of one substance with the tensile strength of another, are already coming into use in the air-craft industry. When such new materials become more widely available, we can imagine that a change will take place in the very design of our cities. Perhaps we will finally see the end of the solid, squat affairs we have become so used to.

DYMAXION

TYPE Suspension
SPONSOR R: Buckminster Fuller
COUNTRY United States

DATE-1928

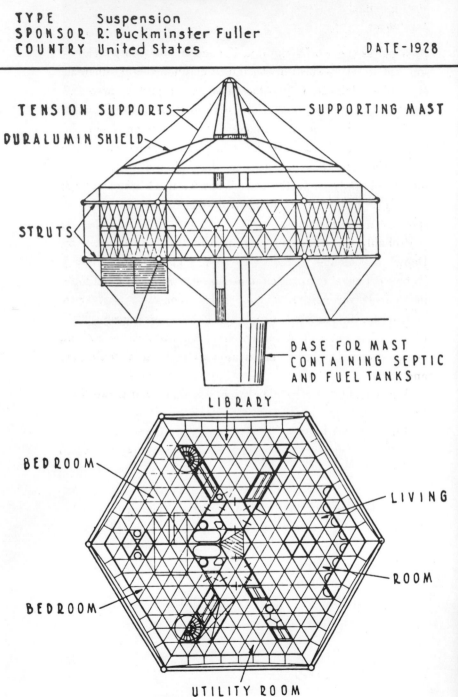

TENSION SUPPORTS

DURALUMIN SHIELD

SUPPORTING MAST

STRUTS

BASE FOR MAST
CONTAINING SEPTIC
AND FUEL TANKS

LIBRARY

BEDROOM

LIVING

ROOM

BEDROOM

UTILITY ROOM

R. Buckminster Fuller's idea for a house suspended from cables.

Perhaps, as the world-reknowned scientist, Sir George Thomson, put it, "The world of the future may look more ethereal, more like a fairyland, than the world of the past or present."

And why can't we, as Dr. Athelstan Spilhaus of the Franklin Institute in Philadelphia suggests, take a lesson from the trees? They grow leaves in the spring and summer when they are useful, and discard them in the fall and winter when they would only be in the way. What we need are structures (like the "insta-shelter" in the Prologue) that are more responsive to the elements.

Probably the last word in responsiveness was forecast by Daniel F. Galouye in his short story, "The City of Force." Here we find a civilization that has developed the ultimate in control over matter. Chairs, tables, food, walls, whatever you wish, are created or changed by rearranging atoms through force of will. A plastic chair, for instance, is nothing but an assemblage of common atoms like oxygen, hydrogen, and so on.

Why shouldn't we be able to control them and make them do our bidding?

Why not indeed?

3

Housing

For Sale: Two modular bedrooms 10′ x 14′. Used only 14 years. Built-in air suspension jets; can be hauled away as is. No longer needed; children married or in college. Will accept any reasonable offer.

WILL WE SEE such ads some time in the future? It is very likely. After all, people become attached to their homes, and will often add one or more rooms when additional space is needed rather than move to another house. Yet when the children have grown and gone out on their own, the house, which once seemed so small, suddenly seems enormous. Why then shouldn't the homeowner be able to decrease the size of his house as well as enlarge it?

It may also be that once he has his hands on a piece of land, he will not want to part with it; for a plot of ground may one day be the most valuable commodity around. Even today an old house in a desirable suburb may be worth less than the lot on which it rests.

Indeed if current world population trends continue, there

34

are frightening possibilities in store. Those of us who own our own homes, situated on a quarter acre or more of good land, may be required to give up some of this land. Or laws might be passed requiring us to permit building on our lots, or requiring blocks of private housing to be torn down and replaced by multifamily housing.

This would hit Americans harder than residents of other countries. Thanks largely to our frontier and agricultural beginnings, our open spaces, and our great prosperity, we have the highest percentage of home owners in the world. Something like half of all Americans own their own home, and the number is increasing.

Even highly urban New York City was originally populated with single-family homes. Then, with pressures of an expanding population, several families often occupied a house originally built for one. The first true tenement, i.e., multifamily house, was not built until 1838. Fifty years later half the inhabitants of the city were living in apartments. These early tenements were mere dormitories; whatever plumbing there was, including toilets, was outside in the yards.

In industrial parts of Europe, which have been densely populated for centuries, home ownership is more rare. In England, for example, the most widely used dwelling is the semi-detached house; indeed the three-bedroom type is often called the "Universal Plan." The semi-detached house is a single building that houses two families, side-by-side. That is, the two houses are complete and separate, but they share a common side wall. There are several advantages to this arrangement. Less land is used to house the two families and the building is obviously cheaper to build and maintain since there are two fewer exterior walls exposed to the elements

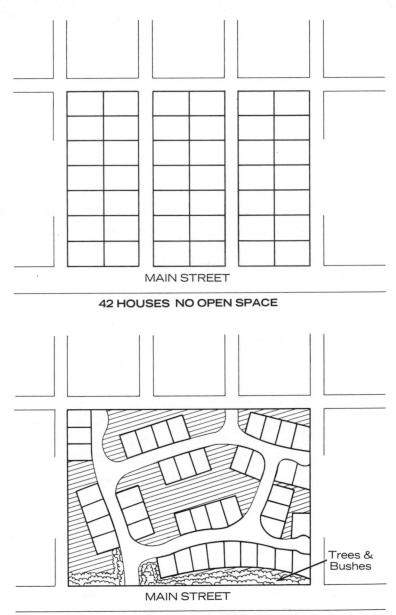

MAIN STREET

42 HOUSES   NO OPEN SPACE

MAIN STREET

Trees &
Bushes

42 HOUSES LOTS OF OPEN SPACE

Spacious, air-conditioned town houses with private patios in the back combine the advantages of the suburbs with those of the city.

(e.g., there is no heat loss through the common wall). Each family is surrounded on three sides by open space. The loss of the fourth side, which is often nothing more than an unattractive alley in American development, is not a great one. And, finally, the semi-detached house, being basically cheaper, can be built of more substantial materials such as brick or stone, and can have more attention paid to its architecture for the same price.

Another way to utilize land more efficiently is to cluster single-family houses on *smaller* plots; but this is done in such a way that the illusion of space is created by the clustering. Further, the land that is saved is left as open space which is usable by all. These spaces are generally maintained by professional gardeners. Often they are the more attractive parts of the area, with brooks, hummocks, clusters of trees, and so on.

An extension of the semi-detached variety is the row house. In the United States, where it is becoming quite popular, it is called the town house. Again, each family owns its own home, but it is part of a row of such houses. In some of its better applications it is designed in such a way that thirty or forty such houses are grouped, usually in units of five or six, around a "village green." This semi-enclosed area then becomes a focus for neighborhood activities and gives the residents a feeling of community spirit. It can also, thanks to frugal use of land, provide cooperative facilities such as a pool, tennis and handball courts, playgrounds, and so on.

While this is not often possible in the heart of the city, the town house can still provide gracious living and has shown itself to be an increasingly desirable form of city housing. In a San Francisco housing development offering both high-rise apartments and two-story town houses, a decided preference was shown for the latter.

Some Prefer Apartments

There are those who would rather not fuss with repairs, painting, mowing, and so on. William H. Whyte, an editor of *Fortune* magazine and an ardent conservationist, points out that "the suburban lawn may be the salvation of the city," for it is a source of constant work and aggravation to many homeowners, and is often given as the reason for returning to the city. One study made by a Manhattan real estate firm in 1967 showed that fully 20 per cent of the people leasing apartments in that borough were returnees from the suburbs.

For such people, and there are many of them, apartments are the only real answer. This holds too for many single and old people, and couples without children.

Another important factor is economics. During the last

generation, the admitted desire of the average American to own his own home has been abetted by credit and tax policies. The homeowner, for example, is allowed full deductions on his income tax return for the interest charges and real estate taxes he pays. Future urban populations may not be permitted this luxury.

Most people would look upon greater numbers of people in the suburbs as an unmitigated disaster. But at least a few city planners feel that higher densities of population in and around cities, far from being undesirable, are the best thing that could happen.

The world's tallest apartment building soars 70 stories into the air from the shore of Lake Michigan.

It is important to note, however, that higher density does not necessarily mean overcrowding. The latter, which refers to too many people living in one living unit, is indeed unpleasant, unhealthful, and conducive to slum and blight conditions. The National Commission on Urban Problems suggests that anything over one person per room can be considered crowding, while the census definition calls more than 1.5 persons per room overcrowding. Nor can crowding be considered a purely urban problem. One study showed a higher percentage of crowding in rural non-farm areas than in cities. On the other hand, one can live quite happily and comfortably in a high density area without being in the least overcrowded. As a matter of fact, the highest density area in San Francisco, North Beach—Telegraph Hill, is also considered one of the most desirable areas in which to live.

Jane Jacobs, whose book *The Death and Life of Great American Cities* is highly recommended reading, points out that "overcrowding at low densities may be even more depressing and destructive than overcrowding at high densities, because at low densities there is less public life as a diversion and escape, and as a means, too, for fighting back politically at injustices and neglect." It is the high density of population in a city that makes the variety, the jobs, the subways possible. Mrs. Jacobs adds that low densities (e.g. six to ten dwellings per acre*) are fine for non-urban areas, and high densities (e.g., 200 dwellings per acre) are perfectly satisfactory for city living; it is what she calls the in-between densities that cause trouble. These have, for example, not enough people to support a good rapid transit system, but

* An acre is 43,560 square feet or an area slightly larger than a 200-foot square lot. There are 640 acres to the square mile.

enough so that traffic congestion arises from too many cars. A high density of population can also produce a safe area in that there are always enough responsible people around, such as store-owners, to deter juvenile and adult delinquency. Hong Kong, with up to 2,800 persons to the acre, is one of the most densely populated cities on earth; yet it is said to have a lower crime and disease rate than many less congested areas in the United States.

Nevertheless, there are those who vigorously dispute the advantages of high densities. Sir Frederick Gibberd, the architect and town planner, feels that even sixty dwellings (200 persons) per acre is just too much. And Lewis Mumford, author, scholar and university professor, sets a limit at 125–150 persons per acre.

We shall hear later of a number of schemes for reducing the populations of cities by tearing down and/or "thinning out," inner cities. This might well be a mistake. Nor is the answer to simply build the high rise apartment projects we see so much of. These, incidentally, do *not* produce high densities of population. They are sometimes built on as little as 15 per cent of the land, and equally often they provide fewer dwelling units than were torn down to provide the space for them.

What advantages are gained? One is open space. And everyone knows how desirable open space is. But attend a party in a large house and you will often see most of the people clustered in one small area. Much depends on how the open space is used. Look at the open land around a housing project and you will often see just that—open land. Most of the children will be riding their bikes or roller skating in the cramped, paved parking lot—the ones who are old enough to have a choice anyway. Further, the "open space" will often have big signs saying "Keep Off!"

It is not surprising, suggests Jill Craigie in the Israeli magazine *Technion,* that vandalism is chronic in all the big housing projects. As she puts it, "Habitations built on an inhuman scale seem to arouse an inhuman response. . . . Given the choice, people gravitate naturally to places where they are not made to feel like insects; to alleyways, arcades [and places like] Venice. It is worth pondering that in all the big European capitals the most expensive shopping streets are narrow."

As for the high-rise apartment buildings themselves, it has been found that the typical mother, especially the one living on an upper floor, finds it difficult to keep an eye on her younger offspring should she decide to let them out on a nice day.

A possible compromise has been offered by the brilliant young architect, Moshe Safdie, whose well-known Habitat 67 was put up at Expo 67, the Montreal World's Fair. By a clever use of space and design, Mr. Safdie provided each apartment with its own terrace, thus combining the advantages of apartment living with enough outdoor private space to satisfy the craving that causes most people to buy houses. It is worth noting that Habitat 67 was built in the same concrete block fashion as the Palacio del Rio Hotel discussed in the last chapter, except that the blocks were cast right at the site.

A similar project is planned in Puerto Rico. The method is still very expensive, however, and will remain so until a large number of such houses are built, so that the cost of the special equipment required can be averaged out.

An unfortunate problem is that we in the United States have

Habitat 67, Montreal, Canada.

not yet learned how to mesh multi-family housing with single family homes. Often when a builder finally manages to "invade" a private residential area, the home-owners see it as the beginning of the end and look for other quarters.

But, as we noted earlier, a higher density of residents need not be a detriment. And from a larger viewpoint, suburbs are dependent on the central city. Anything that helps the central city, such as providing room for its overcrowded residents, also helps the suburbs. Admittedly, it takes an open-minded person to realize this. Just think, however, of what would happen to a suburb if the central city, which most suburbanites try to ignore as much as possible, withered and died.

It seems inevitable that the future city and its environs will see an increase in the current trend toward a larger number of apartment and town house units. From a small percentage today, town houses may rise to 20 per cent of the market by 1980, with apartments and single-family homes sharing the remaining 80 per cent about equally. There were 1.5 million housing starts of all types in 1968; by the end of the 1970's this will probably rise to 2 million.

Town of Robertsköjd in Sweden. Note mixture of apartments (center and lower right), private houses (upper left) and town houses (top center).

Not Homes But Housing

Another category that is sure to see an increase is the mobile home, of which some 300,000 were sold in 1968. These are complete homes which can be trucked from factory to site. As such they offer the best hope for truly low cost housing in the near future. Although they are not mobile in the same sense as the typical house trailer, larger hauling equipment and wider highways are making possible the direct delivery of ever larger mobile homes to more and more places.

A typical mobile home is 60 feet long by 12 feet wide and sells for about $6,000 completely furnished. Some are quite luxurious; and double width models, which are fitted together at the site, are also available. A major advantage is that an expensive foundation is not needed; a few concrete, brick, or metal posts set in the ground are all that is needed.

Another use for these homes is to stack them as modules into town house configurations. In general they are strong enough so that no special support is necessary. For higher configurations, a simple steel frame may do the job. Eventually we may well see multi-story towers into which hundreds of mobile homes can be "plugged," either permanently or for however long is desired. This could bring the mobile home into the central areas of the city; presently they are more or less restricted to the suburban and rural areas.

Modularization is also beginning to play a part in private home design. This will increase. The prospective home buyer may one day be presented with a catalog of house parts or, even better, a box of model house parts which he can put together more or less at will. The bathroom, for example,

45

Mobile homes can be "stacked" into town house configurations.

could be something like that shown opposite. Homes with movable walls, exterior as well as interior, are also likely. Changes could be made to suit the needs, desires, and even moods of the family.

Homes may change in other ways as well. The private home in the suburb may lose its front door, which is even now being used less and less. (A friend of mine uses the space just inside his front door for a piano.) Children and deliverymen normally use the back or side door, and our increasingly motorized suburbanites often do the same, largely because they are closer to these doors when they park their cars in the driveway or garage. And eventually, when the personal helicopter or jet belt becomes a reality, the front door may even be on the roof!

There will also be considerably more interplay between indoor and outdoor life. It is estimated that nearly half the

46

homes built in 1969 were designed for outdoor as well as indoor living. The future is likely to see outdoor areas heated as rooms are now.

Some forty years ago someone made the statement, "Modern society needs houses, parks, and highways." Le Corbusier, the great French architect, answered, "No. Modern society needs *housing*, parks and highways." What he meant, of course, is that apartment living can be both pleasant and desirable—if the apartments are well designed. His solution to the ever-present dwelling problem consisted of vast housing units. As we might expect, they have been both praised and damned but have, in any case, formed the model for a great number of large housing projects. For an example, see page 83.

An intriguing part of his proposal involved the absence or reduction of individual kitchens. He suggested having caterers do all the buying of food and serving of most meals. He pointed out (in his book *The Radiant City*) that "It is by organizing communal services that the city dweller will avoid pointless fatigue."

The reason I called this part of his proposal intriguing is

Modular bathroom of the future.

that an experimental project of this type is actually being built in Moscow today. Two 16-story apartment buildings will contain 812 apartments but no kitchens! All the residents will take their meals in communal dining rooms. Should a family wish to eat in their apartment they will be able to order food from the central kitchen. In addition, each apartment will have a small refrigerator and two-burner stove for snacks.

The communal aspects are being carried still further. There will, for instance, be little storage and closet space in each apartment; many of the items normally kept by the individual families will be held in a special area. Even outer garments will be left in a downstairs public check room. Each floor will also have its own self-service clothes washers and dryers, and even communal ironing boards.

There will also be a community center which includes a pool, gymnasium, sauna, day care center for youngsters, theater, library, a photo lab for hobbyists, and even a glassed-in garden.

Will this be the apartment house of the future? Who can say? The brilliant writer H. G. Wells, whose dozens of science fiction books have fascinated millions, looked often into the future. In *When the Sleeper Wakes* (1899) he saw "that London, regarded as a living place, was no longer an aggregation of houses but a prodigious hotel, an hotel with a thousand classes of accommodation, thousands of dining halls, chapels, theatres, markets and places of assembly. . . ."

Clearly the final picture of the home of the future, if there is one, is not yet in. But if, in addition to considering the problem of providing decent housing for all, we recall that the average person of today spends 75 per cent of his time at home, we realize just how important a part of a city its housing is.

4

The City Goes Indoors

IT IS COLD and windy; a mixture of freezing rain and snow is blowing in Mrs. Smith's face. This is no day to be out but she has been busy all week and simply has to get some things for her dinner party that night. She has parked the car in the Downtown Parking lot and is now trudging the two blocks to Johnson's Card and Party Shop. "Look out!" someone shouts. "That car is going to splash you!" Too late. She arrives at Johnson's wet and miserable. It is too warm in there. She takes off her coat and lugs it around. . . .

The scene shifts to a suburban shopping center. Here things are a little better in that she can park closer to the store of her choice, and once in the shopping center she is less likely to have to battle cars in her trip from store to store. However, she knows too that in general the shopping center does not contain the variety of goods that one can find in a good downtown area. One of the problems is that shopping centers serve only a single type of buyer, namely the residential, while downtown areas cater to business, commercial, entertainment, and a host of other types of buyers, as well as the residential inhabitant. With a larger, more diversified set of customers, the downtown stores can obviously offer a wider selection of goods.

What then is the answer? One approach is the downtown department store. Here one can obtain almost anything, except perhaps items of a highly specialized nature. Macy's department store in Queens, New York, has wrapped its parking lot around the store. Thus not only is the shopper protected from the elements, but she can park near the desired department as well.

The idea of protecting the shopper from the elements is catching on. A number of shopping centers, both in and out of cities, have been fully enclosed. Thus once the shopper enters she is fully protected and can shop in comfort. If the center can arrange indoor parking, which a few have already done, she can leave her outer garments in the car, or check them as she enters. Naturally climate control refers to summer as well as winter elements. (Until the introduction of air conditioning in the 1920's, it had been customary for theaters to close during the hot summer months.)

Rockefeller Center in New York City, although best known for its beautifully planned and executed exterior, has a series of basement level passageways that connect the various buildings to each other and to the subway stop as well. The concourse is pleasant and well-lighted and is lined with shops of all kinds. Another good example is the Sharpstown Shopping Center in Houston, Texas, shown here.

Pittsburgh's Allegheny Center is a newly developed com-

Shoppers can ignore bad weather at the Sharps-
town shopping center.

mercial complex in the heart of Pittsburgh. Here the mall is
an all-weather enclosed area with shops along the sides and
a department store at each end. The area is accessible from
the street as well as by means of escalators from three parking levels below. Thus parking (with a 2,800 car capacity)
is very convenient to the various stores. Delivery service to
the stores is equally convenient, for there is a truck loading
tunnel directly under them. The 600-foot-long mall is two
stories high, with offices as well as shops on the upper level.

New materials and techniques, a few of which we mentioned
in Chapter 2, promise a new world altogether. With already
available precast concrete beams that span 100 feet, cable-
hung roofs that span 420 feet (the new Madison Square

Garden in New York City) and air-supported structures, the possibility of enclosing larger and larger areas becomes possible.

Consider, for example, the Texas home of the baseball Astrojets. The Houston Astrodome is 642 feet in diameter and 208 feet high. No longer need a fan go to the trouble of attending a game only to have it called because of rain. No longer need a game or other special event be canceled because of "inclement weather." No longer need fans in the bleachers swelter in the hot summer sun.

Pittsburgh's unique Civic Arena, though smaller, has a *retractable* roof (see photo), thus offering either sunlight and fresh air when these are available or protection from the elements when necessary.

One would think that, aside from such special requirements as retractability, a dome is a dome. This is hardly the case. For instance, the Weyerhauser Company has proposed a dome that would be large enough to enclose the Houston arena completely, with room to spare. With an 840 foot diameter, the dome would span the equivalent of four city

The roof of the new Madison Square Garden in New York City is cable supported. The cables can be seen at the top of the model shown here.

Pittsburgh's Civic Arena has a retractable roof.

blocks! And it would be built, of all things, of wood! Company engineers maintain that the laminated wood construction would not only be cheaper than a comparable metal one, but that it would actually be safer under fire conditions. For the laminated wood beams would char, but would maintain their strength at temperatures that would cause steel to weaken and sag.

One of the most interesting ideas for a dome has come from Buckminster Fuller. His geodesic dome is self-supporting— that is, it needs no beams or arches to hold it up. Rather, it is usually constructed entirely of interlocking triangles. The lightness and strength of the geodesic dome derive from a few very basic engineering principles. First of all, the dome is a portion of a sphere; and of all solid geometrical shapes, the sphere encloses the most space for the least surface and is the strongest against internal pressures. (*Geo*, incidentally, means "earth" in Greek.) On the other hand, of all two-dimensional shapes, the triangle encloses the least area for the greatest perimeter and is the strongest against external pressure. Sometimes hexagonal (six-sided) units are used. These, when packed together like a honeycomb, are almost as strong as the interlocking triangles.

The result is one of the few really new architectural designs of the age. Thousands of these domes have already been built, ranging from small huts that can be helicoptered to remote areas, to the magnificent United States pavilion at Expo 67. A less well-known geodesic dome, the Climatron, is shown here.

Fuller believes that technology has reached the point where we can begin to talk of domes measured in miles rather than feet. Then, instead of enclosing single-purpose areas—shopping malls, auditoriums, and the like—we can enclose whole, multi-purpose areas, even complete downtown areas. Fuller proposes a dome over mid-Manhattan. More than mere comfort is involved. He writes: "There is, for example, no method more effective in wasting heating and cooling energy than the system employed by New York and other skyscraper cities of the world [i.e., individual heating and cooling units plus thousands of walls and roofs exposed to the elements]. A dome over mid-Manhattan would reduce its energy losses approximately 50 fold.*

The savings in energy would mean that the city's energy needs could be easily supplied via the new ultra-high-voltage

* "Why Not Roofs over Our Cities?" *Think*, January/February 1968, p. 8.

54

lines directly from the coal belt in Pennsylvania. Not only could all electrical energy be supplied this way, but since heating and cooling requirements would be vastly decreased, individual burning of coal and oil in residential, business, and commercial establishments would also be cut way down. The result would be a great decrease in air pollution. The dome would also keep out pollution from external sources, as well as the sound of passing jet planes. "Such a dome," Fuller adds, "would consist of a hemisphere two miles in diameter and one mile high at its center. The cost of snow removal in the city would pay for the dome in 10 years." Many areas of the country are plagued with water shortages. Yet rain and snow provide large quantities of crystal pure water, practically all of which is lost in the streets and sewers of the cities that need them. Rain gutters around the dome could collect and funnel rainwater to a reservoir. If an electrical net is added, snow could be melted and collected in the same way. The

The Climatron, a geodesic dome, is a fully climate-controlled greenhouse providing native environments for a large collection of tropical and semi-tropical plants.

dome would be high enough, Fuller adds, that the water would not have to be pumped but would flow gravitationally to reservoirs in Westchester and other surrounding communities.

In answer to the objection that inhabitants would have a closed-in feeling Fuller points, first, to the delights of strolling "through the great skylighted arcades, such as the one in Milan, Italy . . . in which outdoor restaurants and exhibits are practical." He believes that the triangular or hexagonal structural elements, being far from the eyes, would be invisible, as the wires of a porch screen are invisible from a distance. The surface area itself can be of a transparent material. Thus clouds, sky, stars, and moon would not be blocked out.

For those who prefer a breath of "natural" air, no part of the domed area would be more than a fifteen-minute walk from the outside. Other possibilities present themselves as well. The average worker or resident would be quite happy to dispense with a natural view of the blazing sun in midsummer. Just as he puts on sun glasses to shield his eyes from the glare, so too will modern materials make it possible for the glass or plastic dome panels to darken in bright sunlight, and clear up again for less bright days as well as nights. Such glass, called photochromic, is already available in sunglasses.

When the glass darkens, it absorbs the heat rays of the sun as well as the light, which is just fine. For both heat and light are energy; electronics has made it possible to convert both into electrical energy. Many satellites are already supplied with electrical power from solar cells. There is also electricity in the atmosphere, of which lightning is a common manifestation, which could perhaps be collected and used.

Looking at the matter from the point of view of economics, the Edison Electric Institute calculates that at $2 a square foot (Fuller's estimate), a two-mile dome would cost about $200 million. At a population density of 100 residents per acre, which is a fairly common urban density, the cost would come out to about $1,000 per resident. Many people pay this much already for heating and air-conditioning their homes and offices. Others pay even more in premium land prices for the privilege of living in good climate areas like California and Florida. In more densely populated areas like mid-Manhattan, the cost per resident (and worker) would come out to be much lower.

With domes, cities could be built in deserts, in the polar and subtropical regions, and in many other areas that, if not uninhabitable now, are certainly not suitable sites for cities. It has just been announced that the world's first totally climate-controlled city is to be built near Anchorage, Alaska.

In newly built areas other advantages accrue. Buildings can be airier, more open. Many buildings already have large skylights because of the open feeling they give; perhaps roofs could be dispensed with altogether. Even vehicles could be simpler and lighter. Clothing, too, would be lighter, and the unpleasant changes from hot to cold and vice versa would be eliminated. Not only would the population be more comfortable, it would almost surely be a healthier one.

The dome could also play a part in the transportation system. Airports on the dome are obvious. But how about upside down buildings (with the lobby at the roof or airport level), cable cars crisscrossing the interior of the dome, people and freight traveling in capsules through "pipelines" strung around the dome, and perhaps even capsules that travel up to the roof of a tall building and then connect to and continue horizontally through these pipelines?

Global Time

If enclosed cities should ever become widespread, then we just may see a really great change take place. With continually improving transportation, travel between foreign cities will become ever more convenient and rapid (see *Transportation in the World of the Future*, the first book in this series). The The time may even come when no two cities on earth are more than an hour apart. And when that happens, we will travel from continent to continent as we do now from city to city. Even aside from the sightseeing and pleasure aspects, there is the business aspect. The trade magazine *Nation's Business* points out that what it calls "mobile money" is flowing faster and faster between countries. Clearly the amount of international travel is on the increase.

But—and this is a big but—there is a serious problem already being encountered in jet travel, especially among pilots and those who do a great deal of international travel. The problem does not arise when one travels north and south, for the time zones do not change. But, for example, when it is 1 P.M. in London, it is 5 A.M. in San Francisco. Suppose you leave London at 10 A.M. on a three-hour flight to San Francisco. You arive at 5 A.M. local time! Not only that, your body is tuned to a twenty-four-hour day; it is not interested in local (i.e., San Francisco) time. As far as it is concerned, the time is 1 P.M. and you are ready for lunch.

The body, it has been found, does not adjust easily to these changes. The result of the body's trying to adjust to the local time is called "flight fatigue," and shows up as tiredness, loss of appetite, loss of mental alertness, and other unpleasant effects.

58

Should international travel really become commonplace for everyone, it may be necessary to do something about this. One possibility, admittedly far-fetched, is to put all cities on "global time." That is, it would be noon at the same time in all cities across the world.

This is not as senseless as it may seem at first. After all, since most people will be living in cities most interchange will be between cities rather than between rural and urban areas. Even today deliveries from the country to the city are often made at night and the early hours of the morning. Further, city planner Constantinos A. Doxiadis points to the possibility of the entire earth becoming one giant city anyway. He has even given it a name, Ecumenopolis (from the Greek *oikoumenē*, "the inhabited world," and *polis*, "city").

Naturally the question arises: If it is noon in all cities at the same time, what happens to those cities which just happen to be in darkness at that time? There are several answers.

First of all, vast numbers of people already work at night and sleep during the day, for with the advent of electric lights the distinction between day and night became much less pronounced. The days when everyone went to sleep after the sun went down are long gone.

Secondly, if the major cities are domed we simply darken the dome during the day, store the sun's energy, and light up the dome at the proper time.

And finally, it may be possible, if enough energy becomes available, to light up the sky with an artificial aurora during the natural night. Thus all cities would have twenty-four-hour days, just as some cities far north or far south of the equator have during their summer months even now. It is interesting to note that the brilliant but eccentric Croatian-American in-

59

ventor Nikola Tesla, who played an active part in developing a practical electrical system, made this very proposal some three-quarters of a century ago.

A really advanced civilization could then, by control of the weather, do away with domes altogether. Something called the "seed hypothesis" tells us that a small action taken at the right time can have great effects later on. With a detailed knowledge of weather processes, which we do not have now, we may actually be able to control the weather. For example, a few pounds of sodium iodide, when applied to clouds, has (sometimes) been found to cause rain to fall. As our knowledge becomes greater, so shall our control become greater.

A really wild idea is that of a Russian engineer, V. Cherenkov, who suggests throwing a vast ring of dust around the earth as a way of harnessing the sun's energy and warming up the entire planet.

Perhaps the dust particles could be activated in such a way that they darken or light up as a unit. This would automatically put everyone on global time.

What's that? You don't think you *want* to be on global time? Well then, perhaps you should write to your congressman. Things are happening pretty fast, you know.

60

5

Rebuilding The City Center

THE STAYING POWER of the great cities is remarkable. Both London and Paris have been in existence since the first century A.D., and Rome and Athens for many centuries before that. There are no known cases of cities being voluntarily deserted by their inhabitants. There have been setbacks, such as major earthquakes in cities like San Francisco, Tokyo, Lisbon and Skopje (Yugoslavia). But each time the city, and particularly the city center, has been rebuilt.

Nor have war or disease been able to destroy the city center. But that great invention, the automobile, has come perilously close.

The man behind the wheel has come to think of himself as all knowing and all powerful. With willing support from automobile manufacturer, oil company, and highway builder, he believes that what is good for him is good for the country and that if a few cars are a good thing then a lot of cars must be even better.

The automobile has filled the city with noxious gases and asphalt, as well as with oil, tires, bumpers and other debris. Real estate developers find they can make money by leaving ugly gaps (parking lots) in once beautiful streets, reminding one of an old crone with great gaps between her teeth.

The streets are filled with cars. But the cars are rarely filled with people. Most often the cars contain only one or two persons; and most often both drivers and passengers want to get as far away from where they are as possible.

Then why are they there? Sometimes they are simply trying to get through the city on their way to someplace else. But they are there mainly because, in spite of the centrifugal movement of population out of the city, the city center is just that—the center. In spite of rapid developments in transportation and communications, businessmen still find it convenient to be in the center of things; employees who cannot afford cars still find it necessary to live near their jobs or at least near a rapid transit line that connects with their place of employment; and jobs, theaters, concert halls and museums are still placed where they can be reached by the largest numbers of people.

The core area has been important in history—in the sense of being the place where the major cathedral or palace or town square (or all three) was located—and it is still important today.

Yet many American city centers have, in a real sense, been losing out in recent years. This doesn't mean that no one comes to them any more, but that in the normal processes of change, fewer businessmen are moving in to replace those who move out. Although high-rent office space has been going up at a rapid clip, especially in the large cities, manufacturing and warehousing have been moving out. The net result has been neither an increase nor a decrease in total population, but rather a change in the type of employment. Retail establishments have been losing sales to outlying shopping centers. By and large city centers have become grimier, less vital, less attractive, in many cases even dangerous.

Further, except for the very largest of the downtown areas, there is a certain sameness to them. "If you've seen one, you've seen them all." Would anyone ever say that about the major capitals of Europe or the Orient? Innovations in architecture are being created in the outlying shopping centers rather than, as was usual in history, in the city centers.

What to do? Here and there large stores or other businesses spruced up, hoping that this would help. Large areas of older housing and manufacturing plants were ripped up and replaced with great squares of housing projects or office buildings. Or they might be replaced by magnificent cultural centers such as Lincoln Center in Manhattan.

Or traffic planners would experiment with one-way streets, computer-controlled traffic lights, or other minor improvements. But these traffic "fixes" couldn't work in the sense that even if they were successful, all that happened was that more cars came in and the situation rapidly returned to where it had been.

No one, it seemed, had the foresight or the ability—or maybe the courage—to look at the whole problem. And, as a matter of fact, the first major plan for the redevelopment of an entire city center, though admittedly a good one, fell through. The plan, prepared by Victor Gruen Associates at the request of a private utility company in Fort Worth, Texas, proposed nothing less than the conversion of the entire city core (600 acres) into a huge traffic-free island.

The island was to be surrounded by a broad thruway allowing a freely moving stream of traffic so that drivers who did not want to enter the area could pass easily around it. For those who did want to enter, there was to be a plentiful supply of garage space for cars and underground utility and truck tunnels for delivery and service. The original traffic-laden streets were to be converted to handsome pedestrian malls. For those who needed or wanted it, transportation within the city core was to be provided by small electric cars.

An additional factor was to be a more intensive development of the area, making more efficient use of the land. This was to include cultural, civic and recreational, as well as commercial use.

Unfortunately, little came of the plan as far as Forth Worth is concerned. It was just too big, and too drastic, a change. But the "Fort Worth Plan" has provided a model and a spur for a large number of other cities across the country. Sometimes only the mall idea is used, and the results are only partly successful. The Gruen people point out that merely taking cars off the streets does not create a renewal. Something must be added: beauty and utility, as well as a sound, over-all transportation plan.

In other cases, a scaled-down version of the entire plan is utilized, leading to some very exciting developments and perhaps the first major change in city centers since the arrival of the automobile.

Recent years have seen mall projects take hold in such diverse areas as Kalamazoo, Michigan; Burbank, Santa Monica, Pomona, Sacramento, and Fresno, California; Miami Beach, Florida; Atchison, Kansas; and Providence, Rhode Island. In Minneapolis, Minnesota, a main street has been closed to all traffic except buses.

Of all the projects, the one that seems to come closest to

the Fort Worth Plan is in Fresno. First, and not least important, is the fact that a very ordinary downtown area has been transformed into an attractive tree- and fountain-filled shopper's paradise.

The over-all plan, which was begun in 1960 and is now pretty much completed, included conversion of the core area into an 85-acre island, involving both existing and new construction. Six blocks of the main business thoroughfare have been turned into a handsome pedestrian mall with colored and patterned pavement. Trees, shrubs, fountains, play areas and some twenty-five pieces of sculpture make the area a delight and a magnet that has brought shoppers back to the area in large numbers.

For those who wish to ride, small, slow-moving electric cars are available at 10 cents a ride. Renewal is spreading into the surrounding areas, and new or planned construction includes residential, hotel, convention, and office facilities.

But Fresno is a relatively small city (population 160,000), and its problems are therefore smaller than those of a large city. In, say, New York it is no longer possible to think in terms of a single core which can be rehabilitated; there are a number of cores, each serving a different purpose. There is a Wall Street area for finance, a Fifth Avenue for shopping, a Broadway area for theaters and movies, and so on. This doesn't mean that there are no other functions in these areas, only that these are the major ones. Indeed, it is considered an unhealthy situation if there is only one function, as finance is in the Wall Street area. For facilities like restaurants and shops cannot really exist on a single, lunchtime crowd. As someone once put it: "We shouldn't allow all this valuable real estate to go to sleep at five o'clock."

Boston's central business district suffers from the same sick-

*In Fresno, California, a once-dismal downtown
area has been turned into a shopper's paradise.*

ness that most others do. But a spectacular $400 million plan
is in the works which it is hoped will do for the central
business district what the Fresno plan did for its core. The
most spectacular element will be a network of pedestrian
malls centered around the Washington Street shopping area.

One improvement we shall certainly see in the mall areas
of the future is improved circulation and transportation.
While the ideal area is small enough to be covered on foot,

larger areas can be and will be created. For all but the most athletic these will require some advances in transportation, such as small, computer-controlled electric cars or buses, moving sidewalks, minirails, monorails and the like. Further, better means of transportation from the outlying areas to the core will be required if the plan is not to drown in a sea of cars. (Many approaches to the problem are discussed in *Transportation in the World of the Future.*)

Another change that will be seen is a more, not less, intensive use of the land—for example, a greater use of the third, or vertical, dimension. The *Journal* of the American Institute of Architects (AIA) points out that except for New York City and Chicago the average height of buildings in big cities is still only about two stories. And average ground coverage is still only 15 per cent. Even in Manhattan, in spite of the great boom in office construction since World War II, only 5 per cent of the area between Central Park and the Battery is used for office buildings.

The AIA *Journal* points out that full utilization of the land within three or four miles of the center of Milwaukee would satisfy all the demands of what is now a great sprawl.

In many core areas nearly half the land area is taken up by streets and parking lots. Improved public transportation can bring at least some of this land back onto the tax rolls.

As the city sprawls farther and farther out from the center, costs go up due to stretching of services (water, sewers, police and fire protection, etc.); time goes up for the already weary commuter; and congestion continues to get worse. As the *Journal* puts it, "Sprawl is not a flight from congestion but its principal cause."

Efficient Land Use

When we speak of a more intensive use of land in core areas, this does not mean that the entire central core will be covered over with buildings. Rather it means that a greater number of tall buildings will be used, as for example the twin 110-story towers now being built in lower Manhattan. And it means putting to use a lot of unused and *underused* land, such as parking lots, freight yards, one- and two-story buildings, and so on.

Building *over* presently used land involves the use, rental or purchase of what are called "air rights." One of the first such applications was the old office building built over New York's Grand Central Station in the early 1900's. Thus the idea is not new. It is, however, receiving greater attention now because of increasing congestion in cities. In the New York approach to the George Washington Bridge, a large amount of space that might formerly have been lost to highways has been used for a bus terminal and four large apartment buildings.* It has been proposed that a high-rise business and office complex be built over a 15-acre city owned reservoir in northwest Philadelphia. Another example of the use of air rights is illustrated on page 71, showing how a small, but lovely, church was saved in a busy section of downtown Athens, Greece.

Another likely development is greater use of land *below* ground. In a short story called "The Machine Stops," written in 1928 by E. M. Forster, all of humanity lives underground in separate, small cells. All their wants are provided for auto-

---

* It should, however, be noted that there have been complaints from the occupants of these buildings about the fumes from the traffic.

68

Model of the World Trade Center in lower Manhattan. Not one, but two 110-story towers.

A bus terminal and four large apartment build-ings use space that once would have been lost.

matically, and all their admitted needs for intercommunication are handled neatly and quickly by electronic means. Thus there is no need to travel or even go outside. The soft white skin of the inhabitants of this world lead them to shun sun-light—just as termites do! Even the air outside is said to be poisonous.

Perhaps you think the idea of living and working under-ground is pure fiction. If so, let me remind you that even aside from using wartime bomb shelters, a number of countries, including Sweden and the United States, have large installa-tions, such as field hospitals and military headquarters, buried deep underground. Although built primarily for protection in case of war, these are sites where people actually live and

70

work. In Texas a school has been built below ground level and is claimed to have certain advantages, such as cheaper construction, better insulation, and less distraction from the outside world. Underground garages, subways, and stores are of course quite common already.

In Little Rock, Arkansas, merchants have found a way to brighten up areas that have been torn down for urban renewal during the sometimes long period between demolition and start of construction. A "portable park," complete with benches, trees, and flagstone paving, has been installed on a

Use of air-space above a lovely little church in the heart of busy downtown Athens saved it from the wrecker's ball.

block-long site along the city's Main Street, along with the more usual parking lot. When the time for construction arrives, the components of the park can be loaded on a large truck in a few hours and transported to the next site awaiting construction.

By judicious use of taller buildings, air rights, and so on, it will actually be possible to free more land for entertainment and recreation purposes. This may become more of a necessity than an amenity. For as cities become more densely populated the time may well come when "getting away for the weekend" will simply be an impossibility because so many will be trying to do it.

The distinguished French writer Bertrand de Jouvenal speaks of pathetic attempts to get away from it all which "crowd the roads on weekends and crowd the beaches in vacation periods. It shall be found," he goes on, "that there is no escape—quite soon Greece will resemble Coney Island—then it will be realized that what needs to be done is to improve Coney Island."

Downtown areas, too, will have to provide for large scale recreation and entertainment, as well as performing their other functions. One of the most marvelous examples of what can be done in a relatively small area is Tivoli Gardens in Copenhagen, Denmark. Here in 22 acres (compared with Central Park's 846), there are six large restaurants, a dance hall, two bandstands providing almost continuous music day and evening, an open-air theater, a lake, and a world-famous amusement park complete with miniature railroad.

Large Scale Redevelopment

Pittsburgh has long been known for its industrial might; to the outsider, it has been a coal and steel center, and that's all. To the insider, the picture was of course more complicated. After World War II ended in 1945, Pittsburgh found itself entering the modern era with grime on its face, a large number of old-fashioned factories and mills, and a generally poor business outlook. Added to this were problems of smoke and smog, as well as periodic flooding from the Allegheny and Monongahela Rivers.

After years of planning and work, plus about $3 billion in public and private funds, smoke and flood control have begun to show results. Gleaming new skyscrapers have replaced decaying warehouses and lofts in the city's midst, and handsome parks, apartments, and town houses have replaced ugly commercial areas. In a very real sense it can be said that the city has been saved from almost total decay.

Toronto is another city whose center has been suffering problems of decay and congestion. As a matter of fact the city, which had been built on the shores of Lake Ontario, found itself "separated" from the lake front by a decaying area and had been growing north, away from the lake. Toronto's answer is Metro Center, "the largest single downtown redevelopment plan ever undertaken in North America."

The Metro Center Plan has four major elements: a transportation complex, a communications and broadcasting center, a commercial-office area, and a residential area. The billion-dollar program, when completed in about fifteen years, is expected to provide metropolitan Toronto with a new downtown core.

Gateway Center. Gleaming new skyscrapers have replaced decaying warehouses and lofts in Pittsburgh.

Old Versus New

But not everyone agrees that the best way to handle all decaying areas is to rip them up, throw them away, and replace them with some kind of urban renewal project.

Jane Jacobs, for example, points out that a city area with only old buildings "is not a failure because of being all old. It is the other way around." That is, it is all old because it is a failure. Only in a completely stagnant society would there be no need for *constant* renewal, though on a smaller scale, and piece by piece. But developers will not invest in a dying area, and owing to certain quirks in our tax laws, landlords can often make out better with their old decaying buildings than they can with spanking new ones.

All of which goes to say that the most successful areas of the future may well be those which never had to be ripped up in their entirety and completely rebuilt. A truly successful area (like midtown New York) will continue to be renewed and hence will not end up a purely modern sleek area, at least not all at once. Further, older areas have a certain charm which no new development can obtain immediately. Greenwich Village and Brooklyn Heights in New York, Beacon Hill in Boston and Georgetown in Washington, D.C., are all old, but highly desirable places to live and work.

One of the problems with complete change is that almost *any* area has a large number of residents and businessmen. After all, it is often the more crowded areas that are considered the most run down. But these people do not necessarily want to go elsewhere. For example, what appears at first glance to be a slum may in reality be a low-rent haven for struggling artists, writers, and musicians. Until such time as society is willing to house them for nothing or at rents equivalent to what they have been paying, it might be heartless and thoughtless to turn them out in favor of a housing project (usually costing more than the present tenants can afford) or an office building. Sometimes it is not even a question of economics; many artists who require a lot of space and light and high ceilings have found that the best possible space they can obtain is a loft in an old warehouse or factory.

So redevelopment often brings with it serious problems of relocation. These are rarely thought of by outsiders who see only a picture of a magnificent new office/entertainment/residential complex. Nor do they consider that it is most often the poor who are being displaced, and that it is the poor who have the most trouble finding places to live.

In terms of housing there was for a while a general feeling that the best thing to do was to replace old neighborhoods with large apartment projects. But the results were often sterile and posed difficult relocation problems for residents

Site of Metro Center today.

and businessmen. There seems to be a change of heart taking place, with more emphasis being placed on the possible rehabilitation of existing private housing, and slightly less on the constant building of public housing. Of course both are needed and will be used. Another approach, as we mentioned earlier, is better utilization of the land when building or rebuilding.

In Summit, New Jersey, a kind of "leap frog" is going to be played in an attempt to save a decaying, but still desirable,

Metro Center tomorrow.

neighborhood. The plan is starting with a new building on a parking lot contributed by the city. This will permit residents to remain in their own neighborhood while rehabilitation and reconstruction of their old buildings takes place.

The term "urban renewal" was coined only about a decade ago, although of course it has been going on as long as cities have been in existence. But now, with rapidly increasing urban populations, and just as rapidly increasing expectations of the poor, the job has increased fantastically in magnitude;

Proposed rehabilitation of Harlem apartments leaves neighborhood intact.

and it is probable that most of it will have to be done by means of large scale projects. In cities across the country, a start has been made. We have mentioned a few examples; others are Penn Center in Philadelphia and Century City in Los Angeles. And plans are in the works for many more. Congress is supporting many of these plans through the Model Cities program, enacted in 1966.

We have used the words "plan" and "planning" in a rather vague way up to now. But who really decides which slums to rip out, where to put that major highway, where to put the apartments and where the jobs, how much land to allocate to each, and where to build the cultural center, if at all?

Who makes these decisions today and how are they made? How will they be made in the future? To learn something about this, we turn now to the complex, tricky process called city planning.

6

Planning

MODERN SOCIETY IS changing from an industrial to a post-industrial economy. All this means is that the focus of attention in our economy is changing from "blue collar" operations such as manufacturing and warehousing to "white collar" operations like banking, advertising, insurance, and so on. This change is nowhere seen more clearly than in the apparently insatiable demand for office space in the major cities of the world.

In Manhattan alone some five million square feet of office space was opened for business in 1968. Every square foot of it had been rented before completion. The next few years are expected to see an average of ten million square feet each year, most of which has already been rented. Since World War II, New York has built more office space than the next twenty-two largest cities in the United States; and over the next several years this one city is expected to account for fully one-third of the world total!

Because demand for office space is so strong in New York, and particularly in Manhattan, it is instructive to look more carefully at the situation there. The real estate developers, who stand to gain the most from the great demand, will naturally build all they can, and wherever they can. Because of this they can offer high prices for older properties. One sad example is the once famous Astor Hotel, long a Manhattan landmark, which has recently been torn down, to be replaced by yet another office building. And the Paramount Theater, where teenagers once flocked in huge numbers to see and hear Frank Sinatra, has also gone down.

Third Avenue was once dingy and noisy because of the "el" that ran down its wide street. But it was also a fascinating area, world renowned for its many small antique shops.

Today, thanks to the removal of the elevated railway, the street is cleaner and neater—and filled with row upon row of faceless office skyscrapers. The area has lost its charm. That the el had to go is beyond question. The question is, what replaced it? And could something better have been arranged?

Something similar happened to the once-fabulous residential areas along Park Avenue. Handsome old apartment buildings have been bowled over as the powerful office buildings marched relentlessly uptown.

The New York Times architecture critic Ada Louise Huxtable asks a significant question in the title of one of her articles, "Will Slab City Take Over Times Square?" She points out that, although it has its sordid aspects, Times Square is yet a "strongly beating urban heart among cool commercial towers, a night and day world of sun and neon against one of New York's few remaining open skies. It has what planners call a sense of place. Even its sordid aspects [cheap souvenir shops, run-down movie houses, and the like] have failed to dim its vitality as the city's entertainment center or its reputation as a landmark—one of the most familiar in the world."

Would the city be better off without it? Hardly. Is it indeed in danger? Almost all the property surrounding Times Square is already in developers' hands, with the Astor Hotel and the Paramount Theater only signs of what may yet come.

Miss Huxtable adds that the "developers' pattern, if left to itself, is mechanically predictable: the same sleek, faceless slabs that are marchinug down Sixth Avenuc, the same repetitive banks and showrooms on their ground floors, the same impersonal big business, big building mold."

In these large shiny buildings there is no room for second hand book stores, record shops that specialize in jazz, and all the hundreds of small experimental or fringe-type businesses that traditionally make a downtown exciting.

Even the world-famed theater district is in jeopardy. No new theaters were built for several decades although several were lost. The city recognizes this and is offering bonuses to builders by allowing them to build larger buildings if they include a theater in their plans.

This is an example of zoning, the traditional way of controlling and guiding growth. Rules are established which say what kind of buildings—e.g., residential, manufacturing, or retail—can be built in a certain area or block, as well as regulating their height and bulk. Sometimes special regulations are established, such as a requirement for off-street parking and loading.

But this is strictly a piece-meal, and, in a sense, negative approach to planning. Jane Jacobs points out that the worst fault of zoning is that it *permits* an entire area to be devoted to a single use! What is needed is a more positive approach.

There was a time when it was thought that supply-and-demand would be a good guide. The idea of planning was thought of as a kind of socialism. Today we are less sure of this. No one would dream of running a large business without long-range planning. Yet cities were left to the mercies of the "market" and the real estate developers—a few of whom, fortunately, had some conscience.

Clearly there have been city planners for as long as there have been cities. The question is, how much have planners had to say about what was to go on. Sometimes it was a lot, as when Napoleon III commissioned Baron Haussmann to do something about the narrow streets of Paris through which he had trouble transporting his artillery. The result was the marvelous system of wide streets and boulevards that are so much a part of Paris's magnificence.

Sometimes, city planning was a smaller scale process, as in the small, charming medieval cities like Siena, Florence, and Venice in Italy; Augsburg and Nuremberg in Germany; and Zurich and Berne in Switzerland. The secret of the charm of these cities lay in slow growth, during which time those responsible—artists, architects, nobles and cardinals—could "feel" their way. Most of the buildings were flimsier than ours, and could be easily swept away if they didn't fit or were in the way of some grander scheme. Further, social changes also took place slowly; and labor costs were low, permitting craftsmen to devote much time to small details.

Today everything is reversed. Labor and material costs are high; populations are exploding; social changes are rapid, as for example the rapidly rising expectations of the poor; and, finally, technology makes it possible and economics makes it necessary for most of the buildings in a city to be big and

*Co-op City will house 50,000-60,000 people,
yet will be completed in only a few years.*

long lasting. Co-op City, a housing development in the Bronx
designed to house 50,000–60,000 persons, is the equivalent
of a decent size city that at one time would have taken centuries to build.

Clearly planning is, or should be, a different process now
than it was in the Middle Ages. Nathan Silver, the American
architect, teacher, and writer, says that planning "is simply
the application of intelligence to problems of continuity and
change." The big question, of course, is how to accomplish
this. What is needed now is comprehensive planning. It is no
longer enough to say "Today we will take care of the church
and next year we will worry about the housing." Everything
happens too fast. Yet planning today is often done not much
differently than it was in the Middle Ages.

But this too is changing. Planners have really only been

recognized as a separate group in this century. At first they were drawn from the ranks of landscape and building architects and engineering groups; now they are generally recognized as a separate group requiring special training, both undergraduate and graduate. Planners have begun to move out of their back street locations and tiny offices. Today they are being avidly sought and even idolized. Membership in planning societies like the American Society of Planning Officials quadrupled in ten years; the American Institute of Planners jumped from 275 to 4,700 members.

Who are these people? They are architects, engineers, artists, politicians, university professors, and even an ever-growing group called city planners. The big difference, however, between what they used to do and what they do now is a matter of change in scope. Architects, for example, have traditionally been concerned with the design of individual buildings—schools, office buildings, apartment houses, private houses. But more and more it has been realized that each of these structures must operate and exist in an existing (or to be built) "matrix." Just as an individual word may have little or no meaning when taken out of context, so too the individual building does not work, or is out of place, if not designed as part of its background or environment—its matrix.

Different specialists used to be concerned with the home, the block, the neighborhood, the town, the city, the state, the region, the country, yes, even the world. These were the many levels that used to be considered separately and apart. Today it is better understood that each of these must relate, not only to neighboring units at the same level (house to house, neighborhood to neighborhood), but that they must relate to the larger and smaller units as well.

84

Now when a large-scale plan is undertaken, a complete survey of the various units involved is first made. To keep the process within reasonable bounds, however, only three levels are widely recognized: the neighborhood or community level, which deals with sections of a city or with small villages or towns; the city or metropolitan plan, which deals with large cities and their immediate surroundings; and finally, the regional level, which deals with large areas. This last might be a geographical region like a river valley, or it might be comprised of one or more states, one or more countries, or even a continent. (One observer, with tongue in cheek, once called a region any area somewhat larger than the last one whose problems we couldn't solve.)

The most successful and best-known example in the United States of a regional plan is that of the Tennessee Valley Authority. Created in 1933, this independent government agency was concerned with the integrated development of the entire Tennessee River basin—an area of 41,000 square miles and containing a population of 3 million. A more recent example is the Second Regional Plan for the New York Metropolitan Region—an area of less than 13,000 square miles, but containing 20 million. This plan, which looks into housing, transportation, jobs, education, open space, and many other aspects of a metropolitan region, urges the creation of twenty-three urban centers within the region. Each center would include a coordinated grouping of department stores, office buildings, hospitals, colleges, and housing. A draft version of the plan has been published and is listed in the Bibliography; it is well worth reading.

The Time Element

City planner William L. Pereira points out that planning
for the present is futile; it is already too late. In other words,
the time element as well as the space element must be considered in planning. This means looking into the future, trying to foresee what will happen then, and planning now for
the best results at that time.

Of course no one knows for certain what the future will
bring. One favorite method of looking into future is to
extrapolate from the past. That is, one looks for trends in
past events and carries them forward into the future. We
did this early in the book when we said that by the year 2000,
the population of the United States will be 300 million. Perhaps war, starvation or population control will prevent this
from happening. No one knows for sure.

Sometimes trends, if carried far enough, can bring some
odd results. One calculation showed that if the rapid movement of population from rural to urban areas were to continue unabated, in seventy-five years not only would some
cities grow to a billion or more (which is at least conceivable),
but that everyone would be living in cities of a million or
more. This of course is far more unlikely. (I originally wrote
"This of course is nonsense." But who can tell?)

Still the calculation does show that we have begun to lose
control over the growth of our cities. This ties in with the
rapid changes in our cities that we mentioned earlier. Here
is where planning must play a part. Constantinos A. Doxiadis
puts it this way: "If I asked you to build a motor for a car
that would run 150 m.p.h. this year, 165 the next, 180 the

Constantino Doxiadis reviews model of his project for Accra, Ghana.

year after, you would say I am crazy. Yet this is just what we expect our cities to do—to handle more shoppers, more cars, more people."

It is up to the planners to take a new look at the matter. The old ways simply won't do. They have brought us to where we are now, and a glance at any newspaper will tell us that where we are now spells trouble—and that without some major changes things will only get worse.

We have discussed some possible changes, and we will discuss more. In this chapter, however, we are interested in some of the techniques which, hopefully, will lead to some of these changes.

First, it must be realized that plans, if implemented, can change the future. This is one of the things that makes city planning such a complicated matter. For instance, in 1948 the federal government issued a forecast stating that the following

87

years would see a surplus of engineers. Potential engineering students, including myself, heeded this warning and looked to other fields. Yet the 50's and 60's saw just the reverse take place—a shortage of engineers. It may be that the shortage would have occurred anyway. More likely, however, this was an example of what is called a "self-defeating forecast." That is, the forecast caused enough potential engineers to switch to other fields that it didn't come true.

Examples of self-*fulfilling* forecasts are just as easy to find. An enterprising newspaper reporter, public relations man, or real estate developer (or all three) might cook up an article in a major publication saying that such and such an area will be the vacation ground of the future. If enough people read this, become interested and actually invest, the prophesy can indeed come true.

We see therefore that a serious difficulty exists in planning, or forecasting. What we must do is not only plan, but try to foresee the effects of our plan, and adjust the plan accordingly.

Lewis Mumford says, "There is no use talking about the preservation of recreation areas and other open spaces when the mere announcement of such a purpose is sufficient to push up speculative land values beyond the reach of the state's budget. What we need are regional authorities with the power to put an embargo on uses of land that do not conform to public policy."

While the matter of planning has become more complex, so too have the techniques available to the planners. Computers and advances in mathematical techniques have made it possible to pour vast quantities of information into the information "pot," and to simmer them until the proper (or at least a good) decision can be concocted.

88

Oddly, one of the greatest contributors has been the defense industry, where for the first time large-scale plans were carefully laid out and followed. Systems engineering and project management techniques, utilizing large computers and the most advanced mathematical modeling techniques, have made our missile and man-in-space programs among the best managed of all large-scale programs. In a very real sense they made these programs possible. They may also help make good city planning a reality.

For example, you know that a mathematical description can be written down which will tell how fast a given jar will fill up if water is poured in at a certain rate. Well, why can't a mathematical description be given of how fast the suburbs of a city will fill up if we know how many people are expected to move to the areas over the next decade, how many children will be born to those already there, and so on. One problem of course is that we don't know these things for sure. But improved data collection techniques are making these guesses better ones.

Another advantage to the use of computers lies in their rapid operation. After all the information is put into the machine, we can program it to answer such questions as, "Assuming current trends continue for ten years, how many children of primary school age will there be in ten years?" or "How many cars will there be in the area?"

This is called "simulation." The real world is simulated or imagined in the computer. Thanks to its remarkable capacity to store and use data, the computer can handle far more data than one man or even a committee. And thanks to its high speed of operation, years can be compressed into minutes or even seconds.

Naturally the results are only as good as the quality of the program (the mathematical description) and the data that are fed into it. But some remarkable work has already been done, and things are improving all the time.

Games

Perhaps most remarkable is the fact that dealing with the machines is continually being made easier (see *Communications in the World of the Future*). As a result, computers are being used more and more in so-called "games." These are similar to, but much more complicated than, the familiar game of Monopoly. Monopoly is actually a model of the real economic world. It has rules governing the buying, selling, and improving of property. There are rewards for intelligent use of resources and penalties for foolish speculation, or too rapid conversion of cash into property. Sometimes benefits are derived from arranging partnerships with certain other players. And it includes the ever-present element of risk or chance, as is true in real life.

More sophisticated games have now been designed to suit the far more complicated requirements of city planning. There are two basic objectives to gaming. One is to provide practice for those who need it—which means practically everyone from students to the most experienced personnel. The other is to make it possible for those who are working at city planning but who are not familiar with computers to work with the process of simulation. The idea here is to give planners a chance to try out their ideas without ripping cities to shreds in the process.

Among the better known games is one called City 1, which has at its heart an IBM 1130 computer. The game is played (by architects, government officials, educators, students, etc.) in a series of 90-minute rounds, each round being equivalent to a year of actual city life. Players are divided into teams; some represent city departments while others represent citizens' groups and the mass media. The value of working together quickly becomes apparent; for if they don't chaos rapidly develops, pretty much as happens in real life although much more quickly. Players are forced to try to foresee the consequences and side effects of their decisions. They must consider that a new school needs good traffic control, perhaps even a change in roads to eliminate dangerous crossings, a labor pool (teachers), a sewer system, and so on.

The success of the various team performances is judged by the citizens' groups and the mass media who also, as in real life, participate to a greater or lesser extent in the planning processes themselves.

In the Cornell Land Use Game (CLUG), the players are real estate developers who both cooperate and compete with

The Cornell Land Use Game.

other players. The city that eventually arises is in each case an idealized city. Another game, Metropolis, is, on the other hand, a simulation of an existing city, East Lansing, Michigan, and it adds to the land developer the politician and the urban administrator.

Some of the games are simple enough (though still far more complex than Monopoly) that local residents can also play. This may pay off in several ways. It used to be thought, for example, that planners knew what was good for the "faceless" inhabitants of a neighborhood or even a city. Someone decided, say, that it would be a good idea to tear down "that old neighborhood" and replace it with a shopping area, or cultural center, or office complex, or what have you. But this is happening less and less today. The residents are beginning to be both seen and heard. This obviously has its bad as well as good points. Clearly it is good if they are interested in their areas. On the other hand, it is also clear that no major decision can ever be to the advantage of everyone concerned. With more people having a say in the matter, arriving at decisions will become harder and harder.

The despot of old could clean out an area in a week, could order a new temple or cathedral or city square—or even a new city—to be built. Today the "squandering" of money, real or imagined, is watched very carefully. Should someone suggest building a monument or some other "useless" structure, others are sure to raise an outcry and point out that the money would be better spent if it provided houses or hospitals for the poor. Yet the ideal city cannot only be utilitarian. Prisons and hospitals must be clean and well run; but they are not what make up the spirit and the beauty of a city. Can anyone imagine Paris without the Eiffel Tower or the Arc

92

A city is not just housing, industry, schools and hospitals. St. Louis, Missouri's 630-foot Gateway Arch.

de Triomphe, or New York without the Statue of Liberty?

Perhaps, then, games can serve a double purpose. Through their use neighborhood representatives can learn more about city planning and can make useful (valuable) suggestions.

Also, by involving the residents, and by showing the various results of various courses of action, it may become more likely that the residents, once decisions are made, will go along with them rather than obstruct them. A good example of the latter is the infamous case of the Columbia University gymnasium that was actually going to serve the neighborhood residents as well as the university students, but was going to be built on park land. Strong objections from neighborhood residents eventually brought construction to a halt.

93

Since the future is, to some extent anyway, in our hands, it behooves us to look into the question of whether there should be a deliberate national policy to steer future generations away from the ever growing urban cores. That is, should the government use some or all of the tools at its command— tax incentives, monetary grants, investments in housing or industry, or even actual building—to promote growth in the rural rather than urban areas?

In Great Britain, for example, there has been a concerted effort to do this very thing. Since World War II, some two dozen "new towns" have been built or are in the process.

In the next chapter we look more closely at these new communities, and at new towns and new cities in other parts of the world as well.

7

New Towns,
New Cities

IN A CERTAIN SENSE, namely by comparison with the multi-thousand-year-old cities of Europe and the Orient, *all* the cities of the United States are new cities. Further, names like Villeneuve, Neustadt, Neapolis, and Novgorod—and New City —have been used around the world for centuries.

Yet there are certain basic differences between these "new" cities and what we mean by the expression. The British, who have been the leaders in the development of new towns and new cities, use the following statement (from the New Towns Act of 1946) as a sort of guideline:

> . . . a New Town is an independent, relatively self-contained, planned community of a size large enough to support a range of housing types and to provide economic opportunity within its borders for the employment of its residents. It is large enough to support a balanced range of public facilities and social and cultural opportunities. It is sur-

rounded by a green belt of open space which serves to relate
it directly to the surrounding countryside and to limit its
size within a predetermined range regarding both population
and area. Within reasonable limits the proportions of the
total area to be used for industrial, commercial [and] residential [purposes], public facilities, and open space are
specified during the planning process. The desired density
of population overall and its relationship to open space are
also provided for. New Towns are started on previously undeveloped land and are built by staged development over a
period of time.

Clearly, a major reason for building new towns is to provide decent living accommodations for the residents. For example, in a few of these communities it has been possible,
through a cleverly designed system of pedestrian paths and
underpasses, to separate pedestrians completely from automobile traffic.

But an even more basic objective of the British government
has been to limit the growth of the great cities, especially
London, by housing the overspill in separate, small cities
rather than allowing the city itself to simply grow larger and
larger.

Attempts to halt the growth of big cities—and small ones
—have been going on since the first large settlements came
into being. Queen Elizabeth, for example, decreed in the
sixteenth century that no more building should take place
within three miles of London's perimeter.

That decree didn't work; and in this sense the new towns
aren't working either. This does not mean that they have
not been a great success in drawing both residents and industry; they have. But the basic objective, remember, was to
draw people out of the big cities to reduce overcrowding.

96

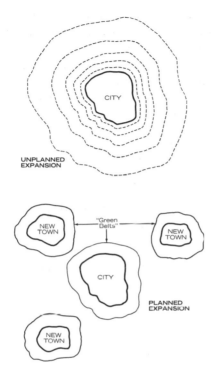

The trouble is that the new towns have been such a success that they have drawn people not only from the big cities but from all over Great Britain. Further, a galloping rise in population is causing rapid growth in both London and the new towns so that there is a continuing problem of overcrowding as well as a denuding of the rural districts. In a certain sense, we are back where we were in the beginning.

Ebenezer Howard, whose book *Garden Cities of Tomorrow* (1902) was to have great influence on the New Towns movement, thought that a population of about 30,000 would be a good number for each new community. The New Towns pro-

97

gram started a quarter of a century ago with a stated population limit of 50,000 to 60,000, but this has subsequently been raised to 100,000, with 140,000 being considered in one case.*
Already Birmingham (not a new town), with a population of over 1 million, has had to use 1,540 acres of the carefully guarded green belt surrounding it for housing.

Other countries have also built new towns, some of the more successful of which are Täby, Farsta and Vällingby in Sweden, and Tapiola, in Finland. But here, as in the English new towns, another of the original objectives has not been met, that of eliminating or substantially reducing commuting by providing industry right in the town itself. There are 9,000 jobs in Vällingby, but most of the people who work at them do not live in Vällingby. Fully 7,000 of the workers commute in. And 27,000 of the 29,000 workers who live in the town commute *out,* mostly to the Stockholm business area. Indeed, the Swedes have pretty much given up on the idea of providing "full" employment in the new communities, which are now called "satellite towns."

This pattern, of not being able to match homes and jobs, is quite typical of all new towns, and many old ones as well. Nor should it be surprising. A relatively small town cannot support a great diversity of industry and commerce. As a result the range of choice is limited and so a sizable proportion of workers are forced to commute in or out.

There might, for example, be only one job in town for a computer programmer or electronics engineer. William H. Whyte points out that this puts the worker in a very poor bargaining position with his employer, who knows that if

* Obviously a community of 140,000 is more of a city than a town. But the designation "new town" continues to be used, probably out of habit.

98

the employee does leave, he must move to another town or commute some greater distance between job and home.

On the other hand, says Mr. Whyte, commuting is not all bad. It is, for some, the only period of peace and quiet in their whole day, and perhaps their only chance to get some reading done.

A lot depends of course on what kind of commuting is provided. Indeed transportation is thought to be one of the keys to improved living conditions. We have seen that areas that depend on the automobile get into trouble with fumes, congestion, and the like. Yet, public transportation can only work when the concentration of population is great enough to support it. Vällingby, for instance, is a satellite town of Stockholm and was planned as a cluster of buildings around the rapid transit (subway) station. Out of the total population, about 25,000 people live within half a mile of the town center.

Vällingby, a suburb of Stockholm, Sweden, was planned as a cluster of buildings around the rapid transit system.

During rush hours there is a train every five minutes and the trip to Stockholm takes twenty minutes. Commutation is thus quick and convenient. In the future, when the 400 m.p.h. trains now being experimented with become a reality, cities spaced several hundred miles apart will still be within commuting distance.

Without public transportation, an employee living in a satellite town can only commute by car. And to make this a convenient process planners must cut expressways every which way through the countryside, for the towns must be connected to each other as well as to the major city. This is an expensive and land-consuming process. An alternative is to place the new towns in a ring around the central city and make the major transportation routes all enter the city, with perhaps a connecting link around the ring.

Another possible arrangement, which is really an extension of the one just mentioned, is based on the figure of a star. Again there is a large city at the core, with smaller towns spaced in a series of rays around it. And again the major transportation links are radial (from the center out); but now there is a series of circumferential rings around the core.

Out of all this arises a simple truth. In spite of all the grand words that we have heard about independent new towns, we find that the Europeans are still pretty much dependent on the large, well-established cities. This is true in the United States as well, where a great deal of activity is going on in the construction of new communities.

100

New Communities in the United States

Depending on how the concept is defined, the number of "new towns" being built or planned in the United States runs from 50 all the way up to 250. One reason there is doubt is the necessity in some cases for secrecy to prevent runaway land speculation in the area, which drives the price up for the developer. The Advisory Commission on Intergovernmental Relations estimates that there are about fifty projects in the United States which actually incorporate significant residential, commercial and industrial features (as opposed to ordinary large housing developments). This figure, by the way, appears in the Commission's report, *Urban and Rural America: Policies for Future Growth.*

These new towns and cities are being undertaken by a variety of developers, including established real estate developers seeking a wider scope for their activities, large land holders, and large financial and commercial institutions, such as banks and insurance companies, which are looking for good investment opportunities. It is interesting that major industrial companies like Westinghouse, General Electric, and International Telephone and Telegraph are also in the business or getting into it. This varied mix will surely produce a wide variety of results, which is clearly all to the good. (Indeed the only type of developer not involved is the national government. This is probably the biggest difference between American and British new towns.)

A number of oil companies are getting into the picture as well. A subsidiary of Gulf Oil, for instance, is building the new town of Reston, Virginia. Reston was conceived by Robert E. Simon (whose initials form the first syllable) and construction began in 1964. One major difference between Reston and a typical housing development is a provision for renters as well as buyers, and the availability of apartments, both low and high rise, as well as houses. An interesting experiment was the construction of two stories of apartments over the shops of the village center. Normally these do not rent well. But Simon wanted them because he felt that they make for better architecture than the usual one-story shopping centers.

It can be seen that Simon wanted more for Reston than a repetition of the usual economic successes (and esthetic monstrosities) often found in other developments. But this apparently created its own kind of problems. Even though the early results were highly praised by planners and architects, rentals and sales were generally very slow. Indeed the project was for a time in serious danger, for a large project like this needs a great deal of capital if it is to continue in operation. That is, one doesn't simply build a city. The process is a continuing one, and requires a steady flow of cash from previous buyers and renters in order to continue building.

One problem, which had nothing to do with Reston itself, was that money was "tight" at the time; this meant that it was both hard and expensive to borrow and so limited sales. Further, the fact that the houses were not turned out in a cookie cutter pattern, when combined with the high cost of building, meant that most of the homes fell into the $35,000 bracket and higher. Thus, even though some industry was attracted to Reston from the beginning, many of the employees could not afford housing there. And, finally, the architecture was just too advanced for some prospective buyers.

102

Reston, Virginia from the air. Note clustering of houses at upper left.

Apartments, townhouses and shops share the shore of 30-acre Lake Anne in Reston.

Gulf decided to put some money into Reston to help it along, and eventually took it over "to protect its investment." The result was a change in approach from the experimental toward the tried-and-true. Some planners say it is a shame that the original idea could not be carried out in full; on the other hand, construction and purchases are on the upswing again. As the British statesman and historian Lord Macaulay once put it, "An acre in Middlesex is better than a principality in Utopia."

There are now about 5,000 inhabitants of Reston; Simon's original plan called for a final city of some 75,000. The Gulf people feel this is unrealistic, at least at this time, but have not published a revised figure.

James W. Rouse's Columbia, in Maryland, presents a different picture. It is better financed and more market-oriented than the original plan for Reston. It also gives us a good picture of how a new community can come about. For many years, the mortgage banking firm that bears Rouse's name had financed or developed apartment buildings, shopping centers, hotels, housing developments, even a church and a hospital. Having built pieces of cities all over American, Rouse eventually came to the idea, Why not put them all together?

The area he chose for Columbia was about midway between Baltimore and Washington, and astride a main highway between them. It is an area that is expected to grow by about 1 million persons in twenty years. But it was also a decidedly rural area, and most of the residents and officials seemed to want to keep it that way.

In 1962, Rouse gathered the necessary capital (much of it from the Connecticut General Life Insurance Company) to purchase land. Within a year he had quietly assembled more than 14,000 acres. In October 1963 he walked into a county meeting and told the astonished officials that he now owned nearly 10 per cent of their county.

Still he had to convince them that what he had in mind was more to their benefit than the unplanned sprawl that would almost certainly occur otherwise. This he succeeded in doing, and Columbia was on its way.

As with Reston, Columbia is designed as a system of interconnected villages. In this case there are nine villages, each with an elementary school at its center, and all grouped around a downtown business center. A third of the area is left for natural woodlands, paths, parks, and artificial lakes.

A system of "minibuses," operating on their own rights of way, will connect the villages and the business center, thus making Columbia practically the only American new town not completely dependent on the automobile for transportation! But even in Columbia's own literature, no stronger claim is made than, "For many residents, the bus service will eliminate the need for a second car."

Although Reston and Columbia, both in the northeast, are probably the most widely publicized new communities, in numerical terms California is far and away the leader, with about twenty new communities being built. These range all the way from large housing developments with some provision for culture, education, and industry and intended eventually to house some 20,000 persons, on up to large cities with a projected population of several hundred thousand.

American planners differ from the English in that the former feel a larger grouping is necessary to provide the cultural amenities and the wide choice of jobs offered by a large city. They now talk in terms of a quarter million as a good size, which is not far from city planning expert Hans Blumenfeld's estimate of half a million as the minimum population of a

105

metropolis required to support an exciting and attractive downtown.

Only four new cities are in this class. These are Valencia (with a projected population of 250,000 to 300,000), Irvine (300,000), Rancho California (400,000), and California City (600,000). All are in California; all are still in their early stages.

Irvine is one of the very few new communities which is being deliberately planned as a large city. But it is of interest to us in yet another, very significant way.

It is to have as its "centerpiece" a major university!

This came about in an interesting way. William L. Pereira, a West Coast architect and urban planner mentioned earlier, was brought in early on the planning of the new city. Irvine was to be built on the giant, hundred-year-old Irvine Ranch, whose 90,000 acres make it about as large as Detroit. Pereira knew that officials of the University of California were seeking a site for a new campus. He recommended Irvine, and he helped convince the Irvine people to donate land for the university.

The master plan for development of Irvine stretches over a period of fifty years. Part of it calls for the campus to grow by extending "rays" or "spokes" so that the university and the city will remain closely connected. We shall see in the next chapter that Irvine may be only the beginning of a new concept in cities.

Cities Within Cities

Along with the trend toward building new towns and cities there is another which deserves some attention. This involves building the equivalent of new, small cities *within* or adjacent to, existing, larger ones. In some cases, such as Century City in Los Angeles, or Golden Gateway Center in San Francisco, we are talking of redevelopment but on a large "unitized" scale. That is, rather than a redevelopment project here, and another one there (in some cities there are dozens), the idea is to provide a single area of a city with the same advantages that a new city outside would provide, but with the additional advantage of perfect location. Century City, now in an advanced state of construction, is considered the forerunner of the city-within-a-city of the future.

Plans have just been announced for a smaller, futuristic $50 million city-within-a-city in suburban McCandless township, which is about sixteen miles north of downtown Pittsburgh. By 1975 the 35-acre tract is expected to contain 600 apartments, 800 hotel rooms, a 3,500 seat auditorium, underground parking for 4,500 cars, ten 10-story office buildings,

Model of Golden Gateway Center, San Francisco, a city within a city.

and a large indoor shopping mall. The "city center" will be a 45-storey apartment house topped with a revolving restaurant.

Among the modern features of the development is the name, "Synergist One." A synergist is something that increases the effectiveness of something else when combined with it. The reference is to the interplay of residential, business, and commercial aspects of the development, each of which is expected to aid the others. Some of the buildings will feature thermochromic glass exteriors, which darken under strong sunlight. Pushbuttons will turn windows black, eliminating the need for blinds. The ultramodern auditorium will present various kinds of entertainment and there will also be accommodations for squash, indoor tennis, and screen golf.

On a vastly larger scale are plans recently announced for development of the New Jersey Meadowlands, an 18,000-acre tract of marshy land just across the Hudson River from Manhattan. Incredibly, even though Manhattan is positively bursting at its seams, this giant tract (larger than Manhattan and three times larger than the entire downtown business section from Battery Park to 59th Street) has been used for little more than a garbage dump and a few highways. Yet, due to its proximity to Manhattan, it is worth, even in its present raw state, about a billion dollars. Although not strictly a city-within-a-city, we consider it in this section because it does lie within a metropolitan region and is adjacent to an existing large city.

Definite plans have not yet been drawn, but the most ambitious idea projects a city of about half a million, with jobs for about 300,000, thus making it easily the largest land reclamation and urban development program in the United States, now or in the past, and at the same time one of the largest planned cities of all time.

8

University Cities

IN MANY RESPECTS, the shape and quality of cities have remained remarkably stable over the several thousand years since the first ones were built. Major upheavals —in the sense of changes in quality rather than quantity—have been few. And they have usually arisen unexpectedly and out of unexpected roots.

Transportation developments—the wheel, the locomotive and the automobile—have of course been important ones, making possible a wider radius for the city. The aircraft has insured that no city, wherever sited, need be cut off from civilization. Electrical and electronic communications—the telegraph and telephone—have had similar effects.

The elevator and steel frame construction pushed buildings up rather than out, and so we had intensive as well as extensive development.

And over-all, during the last two centuries, there has been the immense effect of the Industrial Revolution—the change from handmade to factory-made. Many cities and even regions throughout the world are factory based. The immense industrial Ruhr in Germany, the steel areas of Pennsylvania, the automobile-based economy of Detroit are a few examples. Some cities, such as Hershey, Pennsylvania, are completely dominated by a single industry and might be called "company towns."

Where shall we look for the beginnings of the next major change? Let us examine some of the major technological developments that have taken place over the last few decades and see where they take us.

First, what are they? Probably most important is the computer, and its ally, automation. Automation, it is widely expected, will make it possible for a small proportion of a country's population, perhaps as little as 2 per cent, to produce all the goods needed by the rest of the population. The implications are staggering. What shall the rest of the working population do? We, certainly my generation, have been brought up under what is often called the "Protestant ethic": work hard, and your labors will bring you comfort, satisfaction, and security—maybe.

Presently, out of some 200 million Americans of all ages, about 70 million, more than a third, are gainfully employed. Not all are engaged in manufacturing, of course; as a matter of fact, an ever decreasing percentage of the labor force is engaged therein. The same holds for agriculture. So far there has been no drop in the total labor force, for much of the difference has been made up in the service areas: transportation, communications, hospitals, restaurants, retail areas, education and so on. But this can only go so far. Eventually the percentage of people gainfully employed will start to drop, for the computer is even making inroads in these areas.

Already we have seen major changes. People have more

110

money to spend, and many have more time on their hands. The average work week has dropped to almost half what it was a century ago. There is less concern with security, and more with living a full life.

The next point is closely associated with the first. Those who are being thrown out of work are the unskilled and semi-skilled. Clearly these are the workers whose jobs can be taken over by machines most easily. Heavy lifting, bolt tightening and the like are handled faster, easier, and more cheaply by machine. In addition, machines don't take days off or coffee breaks, nor do they sleep late, though they do break down.

Whether we will ever get to the day when people beg to work, not because they are hungry (for their material needs will be taken care of), but because of boredom or a loss of any sense of worth or importance, is hard to say. But it can be said that those who will be working will be the better trained and better educated. Today, in countries like the United States and the Soviet Union, anywhere from a third to half of all youngsters of college age are attending a college or university.

We are also in the midst of a knowledge explosion. The store of scientific knowledge is said to be doubling every ten years or so. This means that educating young men and women will be a more intensive and probably longer process. It also means that the professional will have to go back to school periodically if he is not to be hopelessly outdated in a short time.

In some cases, he may find that his specialty is being taken over by machines. (With the increasing sophistication of computers, this can mean anything from accounting to wine tasting.) Thus if he is to remain a useful member of the labor force he must go back to school and be retrained. Society

111

might take this into account and support him during this period. Today, second and even third careers are not at all unusual. (It has been stated that half the vocations into which people go today did not exist twenty years ago.) In a labor contract instituted at Kaiser Industries, provision is made for the retraining of all men who are to be replaced by machine.

And of course the population explosion mentioned earlier in the book means that increasing numbers of youngsters will have to be educated as well. It has been estimated that within a few decades half of all the adults in this country will be involved in some way with some form of educational process.

What has all this to do with cities?

Dr. Lloyd V. Berkner of the Graduate Research Center of the Southwest, in Dallas, suggests that in as few as twenty years education will be by far the single largest economic effort. He suggests further that most of the population will have migrated to some 150 metropolitan areas. He calls them "Cities of Intellect" and describes them this way. "Each is a sprawling industrial and suburban complex, centered around one or more great graduate universities, which have been forced to provide the intellectual focus that guides the economic and cultural development of the city."*

There are two important ideas here. One is that the universities, having large quantities of brainpower, will play an increasingly large role in society as well as in science and technology. For instance, they will provide our planners even more often than they do now. (Planners today are often drawn from the worlds of politics and business.)

* "The Rise of the Metropolis," in *The World in 1984*, ed. N. Calder, Vol. 2, p. 145, Penguin Books, Baltimore, 1965.

The second important idea lies in the fact that Dr. Berkner foresees graduate universities at the *center* of his "Cities of Intellect." We are reminded of course of Irvine, California. Others, however, go even further. Dr. S. R. Graubard, Professor of History at Brown University, suggests that the future equivalent of the company town will be the "University City." "By the year 2000," he writes,* ". . . the business of certain cities in America will be education, in the broadest sense. These cities will be as different from the commercial, industrial, and governmental cities of today as the latter are from the cathedral towns of an earlier European society. If I am correct in believing that a few cities of this sort will have established themselves in the United States by the year 2000, they must not be seen as displacing existing cities; they will coexist with them, but will have a different sort of appeal for a growing segment of an increasingly mobile American society."

"Why should such a development be anticipated?" Professor Graubard asks. "The easiest answer," he continues, "would be that education, health, and leisure are all becoming 'big business.' It is as reasonable to expect activity in these matters to center in a few large cities as it was for such concentrations to develop when the manufacture and exchange of specialized industrial products were first undertaken."

This does not mean that the University City will be populated exclusively by students and professors. Consider, for example, a medical school in a teaching hospital. Many others are required for smooth operation: maintenance men, administrators, technicians, physicians, nurses, and so on. By the

* "University Cities in the Year 2000," *Daedalus* (Summer 1967), p. 818.

same token, universities are traditionally involved with the science of our times. Some areas of science, such as high energy physics, require facilities of enormous proportions. The particle accelerator (atom smasher) at Stanford University in California is two miles long! Yet it is only a part of the Stanford Linear Accelerator Center and requires hundreds of supporting personnel: physicists, engineers, technicians, etc. These require services, i.e., shops, entertainment, medical care and so on.

A new University City Science Center being planned for Philadelphia is expected ultimately to have a population of 2,000 scientists, and 3,000 support personnel. On the basis of past experience, it is expected that this number will generate 50,000 additional jobs. Industry as well as government have found advantages in maintaining close ties with higher education. The famed Route 128 around Boston is lined with electronics and other science-oriented companies. The major lure is the proximity of such major institutions as M.I.T. and Harvard. Philadelphia city planners hope that, with several major colleges and universities nearby, something similar will happen along its Route 202.

Even in today's smaller cities and towns the university need not be the only "industry" there for it to be the major spark. Some cities, such as Princeton, New Jersey, are considered highly desirable places to live largely because of the existence of a major university there. This is not to say that the physical characteristics of Princeton are unattractive. They are attractive, but neighboring areas which are just as pretty in a physical sense are not nearly so highly prized as a place to live.

But this can work the other way too. An advertisement for

114

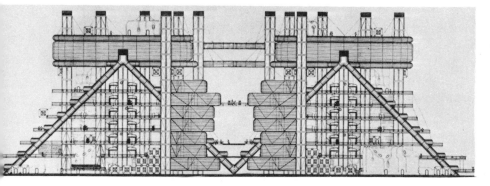

University Node of Plug-In City.

the Taylor Business Institute, a Manhattan-based business
school, starts off with the words: New York City Is Our
Campus. . . .

After all, there is an educational factor involved in just
living in a place. Some schools, for instance, give college
credit for travel. Many schools hold courses in, or give special
credit for, courses taken in other countries.

Perhaps some day in the future, as was true for certain
highly placed groups in the past, no one who has not spent
some time in the major cities of the world will be considered
educated. When Rome is an hour away from Chicago, and
when a universal language (or automatic language translation) has become commonplace, then scholars, teachers, and
perhaps even students will, as Professor Graubard puts it,
"divide their time between several university cities."

However, new ideas in mobile housing may make a different process the preferred one. Perhaps there will be a traveling or portable section of a household, containing clothing,
beds, and other essentials, which will be picked up in toto,
delivered on board a ship, then put on a train or trailer truck,

115

and finally "plugged in" to a preselected, prepared spot in the new university city. There is no packing and unpacking; you travel in comfort and style; and your new "home," though temporary, is almost as comfortable as your old one.

It should be noted that even today the vast majority of those who visit cities for non-business reasons do so with positive, constructive purposes in mind. After all, the meanest town or city offers innumerable opportunities for drinking, gambling and other vices. No, visitors to the big cities are mainly interested in the libraries, concerts, plays, museums, and other major attractions that the small town or city cannot provide.

It doesn't take a large stretch of the imagination to call these instructive or even educational aspects. John Dyckman, city planner and professor at the University of California puts the case even more strongly. He maintains that "learning has always been the most powerful lure of the city."

Why not carry this even further and, as Professor Dyckman says, "undertake the conscious design of the metropolis as an educational experience, rather than [depend] on the adaptive use of it."

In the recent past, he points out, cities provided adult education, night courses, and other educational oppoortunities to aid in bringing immigrants into the social and economic mainstream.

This will have to be extended, and extended far, if we are ever to bring the poor and the hopeless of today up to the levels that the immigrants of yesterday have reached. And we must be concerned not only with economics; that is, we must not give them only courses in home economics and automobile mechanics, nor even only in hotel and industrial management. In other words, we must not confuse training with education. The man of tomorrow will need both. Dr. Robert M. Hutchins, Director of the Center for the Study of Democratic Institutions, says that the twenty-first century will be a "learning society, in which every man is educated not to fit into a system but to discover the richness of life."

What are some of the basic changes that could make this possible? It has already been seriously proposed that all who are intellectually capable, but have not the resources, should be sent to college at government expense.

Another idea is that of "schools without walls." That is, the schools should be open to the community rather than walled-in enclaves of the privileged few. To some extent this is already being done. Some city schools are being designed so that such facilities as the auditorium, gymnasium, library, and cafeteria can be used by members of the community. In Chicago, for example, a new wing of the South Shore High School is designed to "float" over gymnasium and

The Harry A. Conte Community School in New Haven, Conn. In its first summer of operation, neighborhood adults used the library, auditorium and meeting rooms while children from all over the city enjoyed its large pool.

theater facilities that are intended for both school and community use. The school's library is being made large so that it can also be used as a branch of the public library. And an "everywhere school," with facilities dispersed throughout the community, is already being planned for a section of New Haven, Connecticut.

Perhaps we shall also see the present slow drift toward combining education and entertainment carried even further. Will we see "edutainment" parks playing a far greater role than we can even imagine today? Will these be places where, as in the Agora of ancient Greece, people will spend their leisure time in learning, by means of debate and discussion? Will there be studios available for those who wish to try their hand at sculpting, painting, block printing, or what have you, just as there are free libraries today for those who wish to read or listen to records?

Modern building techniques will make it possible for these facilities to be designed for conversion to different functions to meet the ever changing needs of both school and community.

Universities can scatter libraries, studios, laboratories, self-teaching machines and even schoolrooms throughout the community, with closed circuit television or even group courses taught by university personnel. S. I. Hayakawa, President of San Francisco State University, calls for round the clock educational institutions. There is already considerable research being done in the poor areas, which may turn up better ways to help. In a new program at Morgan State College in Baltimore, college credit is being given for community service.

If education does indeed transcend the walls of a schoolroom then another possible step of significance might be the provision of free public transportation. There are many people living in or near a large city who rarely venture out of their own neighborhood.

Free public transportation would make the various great public institutions we have already mentioned available to all. Professor Dyckman suggests that "The partial subsidy of the subway system by New York City makes Manhattan possible; the potential for an extension of this relation is untapped."

Professor Dyckman adds the plea: "As we face the prospect of an increasing difficulty in placing new entrants in the labor force, it behooves us to consider some alternatives to the empty extension of education. Instead of brushing the youth out of sight in rural [training] camps, let us consider placing them in the service of the city."

Surely this would be an important objective to keep in mind when we design "Education City, U.S.A."

9

Experimental Cities

DISNEYLAND. WHO AMONG us has not wanted to visit Disneyland? And who has not been delighted when he did? Most of us think of the 230-acre project as an amusement park, a hugely successful one but an amusement park nonetheless. James Rouse looks at it differently; he calls it the greatest piece of urban design in the United States today.

True, it doesn't have a large resident population; but it has been host to more than 80 million visitors in the fourteen years or so of its existence. And while it has no franchise to operate a public transportation system, its ships, boats, trains, buses, streetcars and monorail have carried 450 million passengers some 25 million miles.

The Disney people point out that there were no standards to follow in planning and building the park. "Whatever worked became the code. Whatever failed to meet the public need was discarded, replaced by a better idea."

The experince gained along the way led Walt Disney Productions to plan Disney World, a city of the future. Contained within it will be a residential/business area called EPCOT—

for Experimental Prototype Community of Tomorrow. The significant word here is "experimental." EPCOT, they say, "will never be completed, but will always be introducing, testing, and demonstrating new ideas and technologies."

For, as someone once said, "Cities need, not plans, but planning." That is, planning must be an ongoing process. The least successful communities are those that have been planned and designed down to the last nut, bolt and fence.

Does this mean that EPCOT is to be a haphazard jumble of experiments? Clearly the answer is no. The city is being carefully planned, but the emphasis is on flexibility rather than finality.

A city, after all, is an organism. It has a nervous system (communications), a skeletal system (the physical city), a metabolic system (raw products in and waste products out), and it is not stretching things too far to compare our vascular (blood) system to a city's transportation system.

A living thing is planned in a genetic sense; but it also changes. A weight lifter will develop large, bulging muscles and perhaps callouses, while a long-distance runner or basketball player will end up with long, stringy muscles (and perhaps callouses). So too must a city be allowed to change after people have lived and worked there and its needs have become clearer.

Nevertheless the plans (genetic instructions) for a living thing are quite specific. So too are those for Disney World. A rough layout is shown; see how the different specialized areas are strung out like pearls on a string. In this case the string is to be a high-speed monorail. The "pearls" are an amusement park even larger than Disneyland; an industrial area; an "entrance complex" or transportation terminal which

The Amusement Theme Park and its surrounding motel vacation center

The Monorail, a high speed rapid transit train meeting the needs of both resident and tourist

Championship Golf Courses Central club house will serve several different 18-hole golf courses.

The Experimental Prototype Community of Tomorrow . . . for 20,000 people, an environment of the future

The 1,000-acre Industrial Park, a showcase for industry at work

The Entrance Complex, including parking, registration center and accommodations

The Jet Airport of the Future — destination for private and executive planes, commercial charters and freight carriers

Disney World contains several specialized areas strung out like pearls on a string.

will include parking, registration center, accommodations, and an ultramodern jet airport; and of course EPCOT.

EPCOT is being designed without a single traffic light in the entire community. This is to be accomplished by channeling all through traffic along a special submerged highway. Trucks making deliveries will also have their own submerged routes, storage areas, service elevators, and loading docks. On the main level of the commercial area, only pedestrians will be allowed. Thus complete separation of pedestrian and vehicular traffic will be achieved.

Still more intriguing is the widespread use of a public transportation system, and a new type at that. The WEDway People Mover (a prototype of which was installed at Disneyland in 1967) is essentially a continuous, non-connected stream of small cars moving along a track. The cars themselves contain no power; they are driven by a series of electric motors embedded in the track. Because electric motors are far more reliable than gasoline engines, the system virtually eliminates the possibilities of breakdowns and the traffic jams that so often result from them. It also eliminates air pollution, noise, and the other problems associated with automobile traffic. The WEDway will carry residents back and forth between the downtown business center and the low density residential areas which fan out from the center. It is hoped that by means of the combined WEDway and monorail, residents, even those who will be commuting to jobs in the industrial park, will not need cars.

The downtown business center—fifty acres of buildings and city streets—will be completely enclosed and climate controlled. At the very center, and jutting out from the "roof" of EPCOT, will be a towering hotel of thirty or more stories,

123

Epcot.

Transportation lobby.

which will be built over a vast transportation lobby in which all the WEDway lines will converge and mesh with the monorail. The lobby will also be convenient to guests and visitors who may have arrived by car.

From the transportation lobby WEDway cars pass out through stations serving office and high-density apartment buildings, and thence across a green belt to the low density residential areas.

124

Business Center.

The thousand-acre industrial complex will provide jobs for many of the 20,000 residents of EPCOT, but it is intended to do much more. It is expected that millions of guests will visit these plants. For they will be showplaces in themselves —not only in beauty, but in the sense that they will be just as experimental as EPCOT: automated warehousing and production, research and development laboratories, computer centers for major companies, and so on. The industrial park

125

will be arranged in the same radial pattern as that of EPCOT and the various parts will be interconnected with a WEDway system.

As with Irvine, Disney World has an important advantage in that it has something special around which to build. The Amusement Theme Park is sure to be every bit as attractive as Disneyland. With millions of visitors assured (and with the Disney name and resources behind the project), attracting industry and inhabitants should be relatively easy. This will ease the "growing pains" being experienced by a number of other new cities. (Indeed the Disney planners have already stated that when EPCOT is filled, another community will be built nearby.)

EPCOT has something else in its favor, good weather. It once was necessary for cities to be located near natural resources and to have easy access to a port or railroad. But with the development of telephones, long distance-high voltage electric lines, cars, and aircraft, these factors have tended to diminish in importance and populations have tended to migrate to climatically and scenically attractive regions. The fastest growing areas in the country are the south and the west. And, in an interesting inversion of the usual process, industry is following the people.

Had someone suggested forty years ago that the modest desert town of Phoenix, Arizona (population then 48,000), would one day catch up with an established industrial giant like Pittsburgh, he would have been thought out of his mind. But it is happening. In the past twenty years (through 1969), Pittsburgh's population has dropped from 677,000 to 570,000, while that of Phoenix has risen from 106,000 to 542,000 and is still climbing rapidly.

126

As the scenically attractive areas and the shores of warm seas are filled up—and they will be—then wholly man-made resort areas like Disneyland, Las Vegas, and Disney World will become more common. Water for recreation, in the form of lakes or ocean sites, appears to have a great attraction to potential residents. But the lack of this amenity in inland areas is no real problem. Many of the new cities, Reston and Columbia included, have built artificial lakes and have placed housing around them.

In an age of increasing leisure, we shall undoubtedly see further development of resort and recreation areas. At the same time Ebenezer Howard was writing of Garden Cities, which had a great impact on city planning, H. G. Wells was writing (in *When the Sleeper Wakes*) of Leisure Cities, which have not—yet.

The Galt Ocean Mile area of Ft. Lauderdale, Florida.

All Alone

So far, in order to protect the large investments involved in building new cities, developers have placed them within commuting distance of existing major urban centers. Columbia is between Washington and Baltimore; Reston is eighteen miles from Washington; Irvine is within driving distance of Los Angeles; even Disney World is only sixteen miles from Orlando.

True, Las Vegas, one of the gambling centers of the world, stands off by itself in the desert, but we wouldn't want too many of those around. Nor, clearly, can every new city be made in the form of a resort area. What then is to be done to "colonize" the rest of the country, i.e., to ease the pressure on some of the existing urban areas?

Dr. Athelstan Spilhaus, writer, scholar, and world-famous meteorologist and oceanographer, firmly believes, as do Rouse, Simon and the European planners, that if a desirable environment is provided, people will come to live there. He therefore proposes to build an experimental city—one at least but preferably many more.

Not a very startling idea so far, but listen. He says we should build them, not where people are already congregating but in the magnificent, vast, unused lands of our country. Dr. Spilhaus adds that they should be far enough away from built-up areas that they can develop self-sufficiency, perhaps even a "personality," and so that they will not be held down, led, or even affected by the hardened practices of dominant nearby cities.

Climatic extremes—hot, cold, wet, dry—should not be a

128

detriment but a useful attribute in that one of the major objectives would be experimentation. What better test for climate control would there be than in an inhospitable climate? We would have what might be called an "'all-weather test facility."

Though the cities would not be built near existing cities, this does not mean that nothing would be there at all. For example, most of England's new towns are built near urban centers, but a few are not. These few were built specifically to house the families of loggers, miners, and the like, many of whom had previously been scattered about in miserable shacks and cottages.

Dr. Spilhaus points out that our federal and state governments have acquired vast tracts of forests and other lands for conservation purposes. Conservation, he adds, "is a worthy objective if done for some purpose. What better purpose is there than providing open space around cities? Such lands would be most suitable for the insulating belts between controlled-size, dispersed cities. The insulating belt would include forests, lakes, farms, outdoor museums, arboretums,* and zoos. Such a mixture would make the enjoyment of the open surroundings not only attractive aesthetically and physically, but intellectually profitable."

Dr. Spilhaus also feels that "When we talk about building a city, we think too much of the housing and often too little of the services to people. . . . I dream of a city where the dwelling units are simple and adequate but the services in education, sanitation, health, recreation, art, music, and all forms of culture are magnificent."

In other words, he suggests experimenting, not only with

---

* An arboretum is a place where plants and trees are grown for educational or scientific purposes.

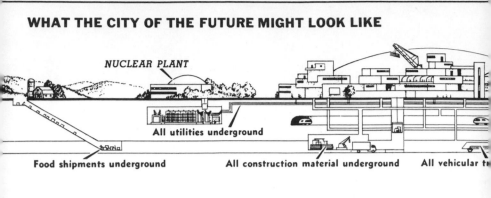

NUCLEAR PLANT

All utilities underground

Food shipments underground   All construction material underground   All vehicular t

The Experimental City of Dr. Athelstan Spilhaus.

the physical aspects of the city, but with the social, educational, and cultural aspects as well.

For instance, consider the long summer vacation from school that we all take so much for granted. Is it really so wonderful? For most children, it means boredom—at least after the first few weeks. For those who work or want to, it means competing with all the others who are off at the same time. But, you say, it provides a good time to go away, which means of course going to some resort area. But it wouldn't be necessary to strain the family budget for that purpose if all the recreational amenities were right at hand—and all year 'round.

Travel? That works all year 'round, too, not just in the summer when everyone is doing it—and competing fiercely for rooms, meals, and space in the recreational areas.

Urban expert and economist Harvey Perloff says that he "can conceive of an effort that would call for the creation of new cities specifically geared to setting up governments that can achieve certain social ends. If, for example, housing were built, with public assistance, to encompass a range of incomes, you would automatically have a certain number of poor people and nonwhites built into the community." Along with Dr.

130

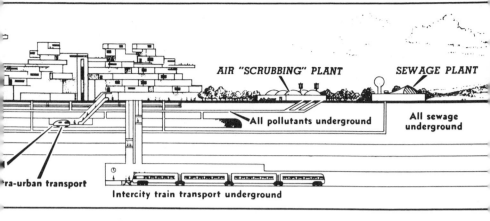

AIR "SCRUBBING" PLANT   SEWAGE PLANT

All pollutants underground   All sewage underground

'ra-urban transport

Intercity train transport underground

Spilhaus, Mr. Perloff believes that "The community could be made so attractive that people would be willing to give up their present more limited advantages to achieve these other more attractive advantages—be they excellent, publicly provided recreational facilities or a beautiful lake, or whatever. You could arrange in advance to have excellent education for the nonwhite and poor groups so that certain of the problems that people worry about simply would not eventuate."

Perhaps a total health program could be tried, including control of the environment. Or the closer school/community ties mentioned earlier, for example, children and parents playing in the same school orchestra, would be particularly attractive to some.

On the international scene, M.I.T.'s Kevin Lynch suggests that new urban concentrations might deliberately be built across national boundaries to help in international cooperation. (There are already centers of scientific cooperation, such as a high energy physics facility called CERN which is located on the border between France and Switzerland. The center is possible only because of the cooperation of a number of European countries.)

The Experimental City will of course be based on the intro-

131

duction of new technology. In existing cities this means fighting unions and restrictive building codes, as well as the normal
reluctance of many residents to try anything new. One major
problem, for example, is the rapidly increasing volume of
rubbish, trash, garbage, and general waste generated. This
comes about not only from increasing numbers of people, but
from changes in packaging. More people buy from super-
markets where everything is prepackaged. The packages must
be discarded. People find deposit bottles a nuisance; so liquids
are more and more put into non-return glass bottles, or in
cardboard, plastic or even metal containers. All of these must
be collected and disposed of. Why not put some kind of tax
on the producer or user of these containers which would be
applied to their disposal? If nothing else, it might force the
producer to find other ways of packaging. There is no reason
why, with the fantastic advances being made in modern chemistry, these packages can't be designed so that they break
down and supply nutrients to the soil when discarded. A step
in this direction has been taken in Japan with the development of a self-destroying beer bottle. Or trash might be treated
and compacted into blocks that could be used as building materials.

Long-range space missions are being planned in which all
wastes are to be used. A method is even being looked into
whereby solid human wastes can be converted to fuel.

The average American throws away about five pounds of
trash and garbage every day! By the year 2000 this figure
may double. The waste discarded contains huge amounts of
useful and even valuable commodities. This includes metals,
the sources of which are *not* inexhaustible.

Why not consider in the early plans methods of reclaiming
and recycling wastes? Much of the pollution that goes up

into the air from factories actually contains valuable chemicals and materials. If these could be withdrawn and utilized, both waste and air pollution would be decreased. With pollution removed, housing and industry could once again be good neighbors.

Many of our large cities have recurring or even chronic water crises, yet billions of gallons are wasted every day. Certainly the water we use should be recycled and reused.

It is only in a new, experimentally oriented environment that such answers to the city's problems will be found. Only there will one be able to break away from conventional thinking and really build the city of the future.

For the first time in history it is possible to conceive of a city without slums, ghettos, noise, pollution, and rush-hour traffic jams. All power, service, and communications lines can be buried or otherwise built-in since the ultimate size of the city is prescribed. A central communications and control center can provide a great range of entertainment and services —including shopping and voting from the home. Perhaps in addition to a sewer system for liquid wastes, there will also be a pneumatic (air-operated) tube disposal system for solid wastes.

Even that ogre of cities, urban decay, can be prevented, since many of the usual reasons for it will be eliminated. And if relocatable construction is used, then even the urban decay that does take place can be easily handled. For buildings can simply be disassembled or perhaps changed to meet new conditions. One planner even suggested "neighborhood rotation." The analogy is with crop rotation in which an area is used for several years, and then allowed to "rest" for a while.

One caution. New cities will attract a rather special kind of person, a sort of pioneer. What works there may not necessarily work in older areas, just as experiments in community child care in Israel may not be applicable in the United States. This clearly does not mean that experimentation should not go on, only that we will have to be careful when applying the results elsewhere.

But then, the Experimental City may become *the* way of life in the future. In the United States alone, population is increasing at the rate of 3 million a year. In terms of new cities with populations of from one-quarter to one-half million apiece, this means from six to twelve such cities would be necessary every year! Certainly, the results of experiments in the first such cities would be most useful for others to be built later.

Summing up, then, we see that the building of new cities offers an unprecedented opportunity: to provide decent living and working conditions for millions of people; to give planners a chance to see whether planning can indeed work on a really large scale; and, finally, to provide city planners and builders with a chance to try out some of the really new ideas of our century.

In the process answers may be forthcoming to the desperate needs of *existing* cities where change and innovation are more difficult because they require *undoing* as well as doing. For example, the suburban shopping center, a new answer to the needs of a motorized age and a shifting population, has provided useful information and experience in the redevelopment of existing commercial centers.

A 250,000-person Experimental City is actually being planned for an undeveloped area of Minnesota. Funds, both governmental and private, have been subscribed for planning purposes, and it is hoped that construction can begin in 1972.

134

In spite of Dr. Spilhaus's optimism, one naturally wonders whether large numbers of people will actually be willing to live in an undeveloped area of a relatively undeveloped state —Minnesota's total population is only about three and a half million and its weather is subject to wide and rapid fluctuations. Temperatures in some counties range from 35° below zero to 108° above. (Clearly this region will provide a fine testing ground for the weather-resistant aspects of the new city.)

But it seems that every area is blessed with something. Minnesota is well endowed with natural resources, including fine, rich soil, "pure and invigorating air," and excellent recreational facilities such as hunting, winter sports, fishing and boating—it is reputed to have more than ten thousand lakes. And it has a number of excellent universities and hospitals.

Buckminster Fuller points to one other attribute that makes it a good location for an experimental city, an attribute which depends on changing technology. More and more, air traffic between North America and both Europe and Asia is taking the shorter, more direct polar routes. Minnesota lies at roughly the center of North America, which makes it a logical terminal or hub for this continent's air traffic of the future.

Airports across the country are already being used as sites for hotels, clubs, restaurants, and professional services as more and more executive activities and professional meetings are held there. Minnesota's central location may therefore permit Experimental City, Minnesota, rapidly to become one of the great cities of the Midwest, and perhaps the world.

10

Megastructures

LARGE BUILDINGS AND monuments have been built throughout history. Usually they were temples or, later, cathedrals and palaces. Sometimes, as with the pyramids, they were intended as burial places for the ruling class.

But rarely were large buildings used for business or housing purposes. This has come about only in the last century or so, fed by the needs of the industrial revolution and growing cities, and by developments such as central heating (1777), a practical, safe elevator (1853) and, of course, steel construction (late 1800's).

In 1865 Henri Jules Borie, a French civil engineer, proposed housing industrial workers in apartment buildings, which he called "aérodômes," that would be impressive even today. In his plans, the great, block-long units were ten stories high—unprecedented for those days, but made possible by the elevator. The flattened tops were to be used by the general public for schools and churches. And—extremely interesting —elevated pedestrian walkways, some of which were glass-enclosed, connected the various sections. The massive planes that the building faces might otherwise have presented were broken up by setbacks which also served an additional func-

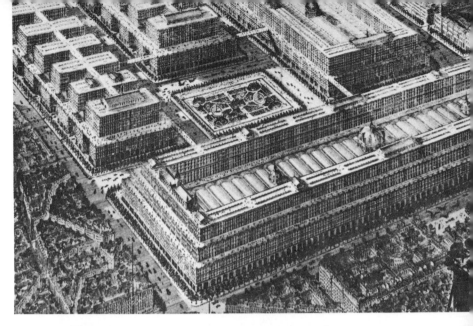

This gigantic apartment project was proposed over a century ago.

tion. The horizontal surfaces that resulted were to be used as peripheral streets which connected with the elevated pedestrian ways.

And this, remember, was forty years before Ebenezer Howard's *Garden Cities* and almost a hundred years before large scale housing developments came into being.

Borie's ideas were ahead of their time, but presaged a kind of architecture that we may well be seeing more of. Not only does a large building make the most intensive possible use of land, but it is the most efficient way to provide climate control. Heat is gained or lost only through the surfaces of buildings. The diagram shows that six grouped units present only about two-thirds as much surface area to the environment as separate ones, and hence will save proportionately in fuel and in heating and cooling equipment. Further, the larger the building the greater the savings. If the structure is large

137

enough to encompass all the functions of a town or even a city, it could eliminate the need for domes, even in the harshest climate!

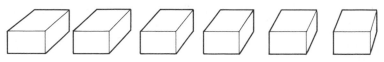

30 EXPOSED SURFACES

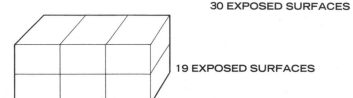

19 EXPOSED SURFACES

Six units grouped together present only about two-thirds as much area to the environment as an equal number of separate ones.

The term that has come into general use to describe such a building is "megastructure," from the Greek word *megas*, meaning great or mighty.

You might think that the feeling of living and working in such a structure would be that of being in a chicken coop. But this feeling only occurs when you are in small rooms, or when you are surrounded by nearby, equally tall buildings. Looking out the window of any really tall skyscraper gives most people a feeling of spaciousness and even exhilaration, rather than claustrophobia. Modern building techniques permit the use of entire walls of glass, which add to the feeling of openness.

In addition, greenery and open space actually become more, not less, accessible, than they are for those living in a conventional city, especially a large one. Normally one has to travel several miles before hitting actual open space. And, of course, as time goes on the situation keeps getting worse. A century

138

and a half ago one had to travel about two miles from central London to reach open country in any direction. Forty years ago the figure had risen to six or eight miles. Today it is up to twelve to fifteen miles.

Even the average new town has a radius of about two miles. How often do you think you would walk two miles to get to open space? In a megastructure, however, you could be literally surrounded by it. The high density of population would make public transportation fast and convenient and maybe even unnecessary except for elevators and perhaps moving sidewalks. Indeed, if public transportation is required it can, for the first time, be designed right into the structure (the Minirail ran *through* a number of buildings at Expo 67) and be a part of it.

Although the term megastructure means literally a great or mighty building, great size turns out not to be its only feature. For example, the vehicle assembly building for NASA's moon rocket is one of the largest buildings in the world. It is so huge inside that special weather control facilities had to be included to prevent rain from forming! Yet it is not considered a megastructure, largely because it is devoted to a single use. In other words, multiple use seems to be a major requirement for a structure to warrant the prefix "mega."

Moscow University, for instance, is housed almost entirely in one skyscraper. This alone might be enough to permit the term megastructure to be applied to it, for it does after all contain the multiple activities that are usually distributed around in various buildings, such as offices, classrooms, labs, auditoriums, and cafeterias. But at Moscow University housing has even been provided in the building for students and their families. Hence one is quite likely to find children bicycling down the halls of the university.

NASA's vehicle assembly building. One of the largest structures in the world, but not a mega-structure.

The planner Edgardo Contini says: "A general considera-
tion favoring multiple-use buildings is that living in a 100 per
cent residential neighborhood is boring, and people like seeing some other types of life in the district." Multi-use buildings combining business and residences also provide a good
answer to the commuting problem.

We are beginning to see an increasing number of bona-fide
megastructures. The 100-story John Hancock Center, recently
completed in downtown Chicago, is a perfect example. This
handsome, tapered tower combines within it practically everything that is necessary for city life. Floors 45 through 92 contain 705 apartments, while floors 13 through 44 provide space
for business and professional offices. Floors 6 through 12
contain garage space for more than 1,200 cars. The lower
floors contain a department store and a bank, while the upper
floors contain restaurants, swimming pool, sauna, health club,
observatory, and lounge. There is even a 900 kilowatt emer-
gency power plant which will provide lights and elevator
service in the event of a power failure. In a good example of
coordinated design, the Chicago Transit Authority has
planned an extension of the subway system to carry some of
the additional traffic generated by the giant building.

Incidentally, we should point out that the term megastructure is a loose one and does not necessarily imply only gigantic skyscrapers or great, block-like structures. A different kind
of arrangement to which the term is sometimes applied is a
closely integrated, connected set of buildings. For instance,
some six hundred families in Montreal can now live, work,
shop, receive medical attention and even go to a movie without having to worry about the weather. And considering
Montreal's rugged winters, this can be a great advantage. One
of the buildings in the project, which is called Alexis Nihon

141

Plaza, contains a three-story retail mall with another three stories of parking above it. There is also a ten-story office building, a seven-story medical center and two apartment towers, respectively of twenty-four and twenty-seven stories. Roof areas are used for three tennis courts, two pools, pitch and putt golf, and a playground. Yet the whole project covers only six acres. (Some suburban townships are zoned for one-acre lots, which means that six acres of land would be used for nothing more than housing a maximum of six families.)

Another, more spread-out type of megastructure is Scarboro College, in Canada, shown here, in which all the separate functions are housed in one rambling, handsome structure.

A megastructure to house a complete city of 50,000 was recently proposed for the Santa Monica Mountains north of Los Angeles. As you can see in the illustration on page 144, the urban center would be at the summit, while dwellings and recreation would be placed along the slopes. The hillside construction provides, in addition to the marvelous appearance and fine views, great possibilities in terracing and sunlight, as in Expo 67's Habitat. Pneumatic supply tubes would provide for deliveries and an inclined elevator would take care of personal transport up and down the slanted structure.

On an even larger scale was an ingenious plan, suggested almost forty years ago by Le Corbusier, for rebuilding Algiers. The proposal was for a long, sinuous building fourteen stories high, eighty-five feet deep and eight *miles* long. Now *that's* a megastructure. A highway was to run along the upper part, while the whole would be built on stilts, preventing the structure from giving the feeling of a "Chinese wall," and providing covered areas for playgrounds, parks, and the like.

The central complex, containing even higher buildings with elevated roads joining them, was to house the business

142

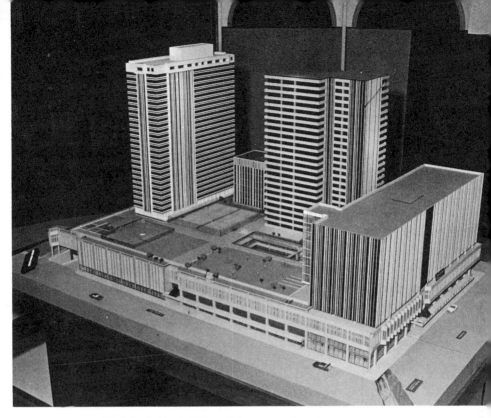

Model of Alexis Nihon Plaza, exterior view.

Scarborough College, a university megastructure.

A megastructure in the Santa Monica Mountains to house 50,000.

section and some 220,000 residents, while an additional 180,-000 would be housed along the viaduct.

Does the whole seem somewhat sterile and hospital-like? It does to us, perhaps. But to the poorer Algerian, living under the worst conditions of dirt, disease, and congestion, it might have provided the only chance for decent accommodations.

But it never came to be built, financial, governmental or other reasons intervening.

As a matter of fact, Crawford Westbrook, Director of Planning at Victor Gruen Associates, says the limiting factor in city planning is "government." Even if the technical and financial problems are licked, we would still have to face the even more difficult task of getting the many local, state, and federal governments to listen to, understand, and work with each other, and with the private sector as well.

144

Along lines that are similar to, but perhaps more practical than, Le Corbusier's idea for Algiers are a variety of proposals that go under the name of "linear cities." Here the idea is to use one or more transportation methods to do for a horizontal form of city building what the elevator does for the vertical megastructure. A proposal for New York's borough of Brooklyn would place housing and schools, as well as recreational and community facilities along and on top of a badly needed Cross-Brooklyn Expressway. Also tied in, as shown on the next page, would be a rapid transit line.

The concept of air rights is also tied in here. As mentioned earlier, there is considerable underused land in a city. Space over railroad tracks and highways is a typical example. This space is being used more and more for schools and apartment buildings. Putting a megastructure over a transportation corridor is merely a logical next step. Two examples are shown on pages 146 and 147.

Ada Louise Huxtable calls the megastructure "one of the most stimulating, promising and problematic architectural developments of the 20th century. Results, in practice and on paper, range from the all-purpose university structure, having a big vogue right now, to Megastructure as the city of the future."

Carried to its ultimate, the idea implies complete self-sufficiency, in which case the city can literally be located anywhere. While this doesn't necessarily mean that the city would have to manufacture everything that is used as well as grow

A megastructure 8 **miles** *long.*

Proposed Linear City, utilizing air rights over Cross-Brooklyn Expressway.

its own food (although advances in chemistry may make even this possible), it does mean that it would have to have its own sources of water and energy. We have seen that water can be recycled if necessary. As for power, it is clear that the advent of nuclear power means that cities can truly be located anywhere—in the mountains, desert, the far north, and even in the sea.

Further, while supplies of fresh water are often limited, there is plenty of ocean water around. Many parts of the world are dry and arid yet lie not far from the sea. Virtually unlimited power makes the desalting of sea water not only possible but, in some cases, even practicable. Hence a number of ideas are being considered for building what are called nuclear-agro-industrial complexes, or "nuplexes" for short. With a large nuclear reactor providing power it would be possible to build a large city in a now dry area; ocean water could be desalted for resident's needs and for irrigation as well. The power would also make manufacturing economically feasible, including the production of chemical fertilizers for the nutrient-poor soil. If the climate is really bad, then mega-structure construction or a dome might be used. Perhaps by the time this comes about, really intensive food production will lessen our dependence on natural soil through the use of food "factories."

Think of the possibilities then. How about spherical, com-pletely enclosed floating cities? A really large-size city prob-ably would not be bothered very much by rough seas. In the event of extremely bad weather, however, we just let in some water and submerge for a while. In the depths of the vast oceans it is always relatively serene.

Does the whole idea seem too ridiculous to contemplate? Read on. You may be in for some surprises.

Crystal Span, suggested as a replacement for a conventional bridge over London's River Thames, would house a hotel, ships, skating rink and sculpture gallery.

11

Cities In the Sea

MAN CANNOT FLY as well as the bird, nor can he swim as well as the fish. Hence with a few rare exceptions he has always made his home on land.

The major exceptions are sampans and houseboats. Sampans are small boats used for shipping merchandise or for housing a family or both. They are used for the latter purpose mainly because the crowded, unsanitary conditions in some Oriental cities make even the crowded quarters of the sampan more desirable.

Conditions in most western cities are relatively not as bad. And so when houseboats are used it is generally because the owners love the water and simply want to be near it as much as possible. Houseboats also serve the same purpose that a house trailer does. They provide mobility to those with a wanderlust—a desire always to be on the go, to see new places and new things.

Crowded conditions on land and love of the sea are two very good reasons why we shall be seeing not only homes but entire cities built in, over, or even under water.

148

An additional point to consider is that most large cities are built adjacent to some major body of water. The portion of the Hudson River that separates Manhattan and New Jersey is almost a mile wide. Hence we are likely to see construction moving out into the river. Already there are piers, heliports, and the like.

But how about a 200-story office building off the shore of Jersey City? This has been proposed as a way to take some of the pressure off existing office facilities in that city and in Manhattan, across the river. We know that housing space is also short in city centers. The proposed apartment and office complex shown on page 150 can house 55,000 people and a work force of 35,000. Yet, because it would be built out into the river, it requires no (existing) land.

That people will move to shore sites is demonstrated most forcefully by the great success of Marina City in Chicago: a megastructure containing apartments, offices, restaurants, shops, garage space, bowling alleys, a theater—and a marina.

The emergence of water as a major factor in leisure-time activities is clearly shown by the rapidly rising sales of boats, water skis, diving equipment, and surfboards. But it is also shown by the names for places that people stay in when traveling or on vacation. The word "hotel" has been around for several centuries. As cars became an important factor in our lives we found "motels"—motor hotels—springing up across the country. The most recent entry is "floatels"—or floating hotels.

The first of these went into operation in the Miami area late in 1969. Attached to stationary docks extending out from shore are houseboat units each containing four to six fully equipped hotel rooms. There are also a limited number of

Battery Park City. Two views.

motorized single room units which can be detached from the pier and taken on cruises at speeds of about eight knots. Except for parking facilities located on the land nearby, everything is floated. This includes a restaurant, cocktail lounge, offices and lobby, stores—even a floating swimming pool.

Alfred Bloomingdale, chairman of the board of the Diners' Club (which developed the idea), estimates that within five years 500 floatels will be in operation throughout the world.

Sea City

Increasing population will bring with it increasing food shortages as well as housing shortages. Large parts of the world already do not have enough to eat, and the situation will get worse before it gets better. For not only do more people need more land for houses, but the land is then no longer available for food production.

About 75 per cent of the earth's surface is covered with water. Enormous reserves of fish, shellfish and even plant food are harbored in the vast oceans and seas of the world.

These have traditionally been obtained from boats and, to a lesser degree, from nets or lines cast from shore. If a proposal of Canada's Pilkington Brothers, Limited, ever comes to pass, a new type of fishing will emerge—an urban fish farm. For what is proposed is a complete city in the sea, built of concrete, glass and plastic, which would house 30,000 inhabitants. Here fish could be grown and "harvested" in "sea farms" under controlled, scientific conditions.

Although the specific site proposed for Sea City is about fifteen miles off the east coast of England, such cities could be built wherever the water is reasonably shallow (in this case

In this Floatel, or floating hotel, everything except parking is on water.

the water is thirty-five feet deep), and where there is a readily available source of energy. One energy possibility, of course, is nuclear power. The site choice for Sea City, however, is partially dictated by the discovery of a large underwater natural gas field in the area. The ready availability of inexpensive fuel, in combination with improved methods of desalting water (desalination), would take care of the fresh water needs of the city.

It is likely that the desalination plant would contain, or be allied with, facilities for recovering not only salt from the sea water, but also such elements as bromine, magnesium, rubidium, nickel, and cobalt. While these exist in low concentration (very little per gallon) in sea water, the vast quantities of water handled could produce marketable quantities. In addition to sea farming and "mining," Sea City would offer a number of other opportunities in boat building, collection and distribution of sand and gravel from nearby underwater areas, and of course tourism. Sea City would undoubtedly be a favorite holiday resort.

Since it would be built on piles, with the sea flowing under as well as around it, Sea City would also be a marvelous site for a college of marine science. A marine zoo would be formed of glass "tubes" through which people could walk to observe underwater life for professional reasons or enjoyment.

Design of Sea City evolved largely as an answer to the harsh requirements of wind and wave. The carefully designed curves of the 180-foot-high outer protective wall would carry even the strongest winds up and over the city, leaving the inner portions relatively calm. As you can see, housing is carried in

Sea City.

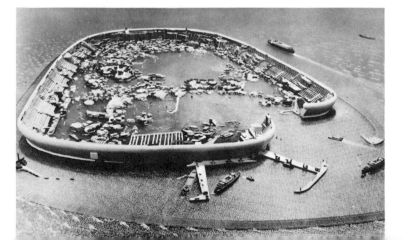

rising terraces all around the inside of the wall, sheltered from the wind but wide open to the sun.

Protection from the sea is afforded by a breakwater formed of large, anchored, floating bags partially filled with water. Tests show that the force of waves is broken before they reach the city, thus leaving a "moat," a ring of calm water, around the city.

When water is used for cooling purposes (e.g., for air conditioning or cooling of machinery), it warms up. It is expected that the climate of the city can be improved by discharging this warmed water into the lagoon formed by the floating breakwater, thus warming it and the air above it. The temperature is easily controlled by diverting some of the warmed water into the outer sea, providing at least some degree of climate control in the city. Or a specific section of the fish farm could be warmed considerably to make possible the cultivation of warm water fish, and even the tropical fish that have become such a popular hobby.

The city itself resembles a huge baseball stadium 4,700 feet long by 3,300 feet wide. Although a portion of the enclosed lagoon would be left open for water sports, much of the rest of it would be taken up by floating structures, providing space for individuals and businesses whose needs cannot be met by the buildings in the outer part. These can be rearranged easily, providing great flexibility. The lagoon would be criss-crossed by enclosed pedestrian walkways, which means that no part of the city would ever be more than a pleasant one-mile walk to any other part. For those who need or want it, public transportation would be provided in the form of a "water bus"—a small boat which would circle the lagoon every five or ten minutes, picking up and discharging passengers at designated stops, as is done in Venice today. Escalators every 300 feet would give convenient access to the terraced areas.

The sixteen stories of terraced housing would accommodate about 21,000 residents, while the balance of the population would be housed on the floating islands. While it is hoped that most of those who live at Sea City would also work there, some commuting to the mainland, and of course shipping, would be required. The latter would be accomplished by standard ships, which, however, would not be allowed to enter the lagoon; they would moor outside the city at piers providing direct access to industrial sections located in the base of the wall. Human transportation, which must be faster, would be accomplished by helicopters, hovercraft and hydrofoils (see *Transportation in the World of the Future*).

Although the cost of building such a city would naturally be high, especially for the first one, the difference between the cost of successive Sea Cities and new towns built on ever more expensive land in urban areas may not be that great. For the cost of the land is saved, as is that of construction and maintenance of roadways. These account for fully 15 per cent of the cost of towns on land.

Floating Cities

Americans are a highly mobile people. About one-fifth of all Americans move every year. And they have been mobile since they arrived in the New World. Often they even took their homes with them. Through the years Conestoga wagons, houseboats, trailers, and mobile homes have been common

features of the American landscape. What we have are portable residences.

Some have carried the idea even further, and have called a
large ocean liner a portable city. The R.M.S. *Queen Elizabeth
2,* for instance, provides living quarters, entertainment, and
work for some three thousand passengers and crew.

Yet, compared to a normal town of three thousand, the ship
is relatively small and light. It should therefore not surprise
us to learn that true floating cities have actually been proposed.

Further, should more capacity be necessary no one would
dream of adding onto the rear or top of an ocean liner. Another one is built. Dr. Spilhaus maintains that the same should
be true of cities.

The Sea City designers agree, and would take care of any
necessary expansion by building a larger Sea City around the
original one, or perhaps a series of similar-sized ones alongside. Somewhat greater flexibility is offered, however, in Buckminster Fuller's latest proposal for floated, prefabricated
"neighborhoods." These four-acre steel or concrete rafts
would be built at shipyards and towed to prepared moorings
near existing large cities. (The Triton Foundation, with which
Fuller collaborated in the study, points out that fully 80 per
cent of U.S. metropolitan areas with populations of a million
or more are near bodies of water having enough depth—25 to
30 feet—to accommodate such structures. At these depths,
building heights of up to twenty stories are said to be quite
feasible.)

Three to six of the neighborhoods, each housing perhaps
five thousand persons and containing an elementary school
and some stores, would be linked together to form a town.

R. Buckminster Fuller (center) shows his model of a tetrahedral neighborhood to officials of the U.S. Department of Housing and Urban development.

At this point, a population large enough to permit proper support of city services would have been reached, and a "service" platform would be added containing larger scale entertainment, recreational, educational and civic facilities, and perhaps even some light industry. The growing pains of conventional towns are avoided, for the neighborhoods, being tetrahedral in shape,* can be rearranged in an endless variety of combinations.

Three to seven towns (not neighborhoods) would form a full-scale city with a population of about 100,000. Again a special module could be added—a "city center," with a medi-

* A tetrahedron is a four-sided solid with all its faces triangles.

157

cal center, a college, government facilities, a shopping center, theaters, and so on.

Should the importance of the city decline for any reason, the usual problems of empty buildings, demolition, and deterioration would be eliminated. (Buildings deteriorate faster, not slower, when not in use.) We simply detach one or more neighborhoods and tow it elsewhere. Each of the neighborhoods, incidentally, is a megastructure. Thus all services, such as water, waste handling, power, heating, and air conditioning, can be centrally provided. This provides two advantages: first, there is no duplication of services for individual dwellings or businesses. (One hundred separate dwelling or business units would normally need 100 separate heating units, air conditioners, etc.) And second, distribution of services is more efficient on a large scale.

In contrast to Sea City, wheeled vehicles would be permitted here, but would be restricted to the lowest level, with all parking in the flotation portion (underwater). This would remove that eyesore, the parking lot, from view.

All dwelling units would face the water. The sloping sides permit more sun to enter the dwellings, and of course make for a stable structure. The front doors of the apartments open into broad, 18-foot-wide "streets in the air" resembling the promenade (walking) decks of ocean liners.

Such a city, having close ties with the existing city, would rapidly and conveniently make additional housing and business space available to the city dwellers. This would not only take the pressure off existing buildings, but could even provide temporary space for tenants and businesses when large-scale renewal is in process. After a city has been "fixed up," the floating city could be moved to another area.

158

Cities In
The Sea

This proposal was an outgrowth of an earlier one which envisioned the use of the same tetrahedral shape, but on a huge scale. Capable of housing a million people, the original Tetrahedral City was to be two miles on a side and two hundred stories high. It could be used in an enclosed area, such as Tokyo Bay; or in some modified form it could be floated out to sea and anchored. Relays of such cities stretched across the world's oceans could provide a haven for shipping in their protected inner harbors even in the worst storms. Their huge size and mass would keep them from being seriously affected by the elements. The seas would then be open to smaller boats which could "city-hop" from one to another. Mid-ocean cargo transfer also would be a possibility.

Another type of floated, tetrahedral megastructure is shown. This time, however, the tetrahedron has been stood on its head. An individual tetrahedron balanced on its point would of course be completely unstable. But when it is locked to-

City Shape/21, a floating city.

gether with others we have a completely stable structure with, in addition, some interesting possibilities in design and planning. The pipe-shaped trusses, for instance, are hollow and serve for movement of people, goods, and utilities. Dwellings, offices, and industry are housed in the relatively thin "walls" of the structure, with terracing possibilities on the insides of the tetrahedrons. The plazas formed by the joining of the "bases" are reserved for recreation, with certain areas perhaps zoned for light industry.

As shown, two rows of pontoons could support four rows of units, only one of many different combinations that are possible in the City Shape/21 idea. I need hardly point out that the view out the side windows would be spectacular; the sailboat at lower left gives an indication of scale.

Down We Go

While Sea City, Tetrahedral City, and City Shape/21 would provide excellent facilities for oceanographic studies, these studies would be limited to relatively shallow water, or to the top layers of the oceans. If we are to establish a closer bond with the sea, we must know more about it: currents, waves, tides, temperatures, and so on. For a complete study, we shall have to go down, down, down.

Fortunately, in spite of the fact that at least one point in the ocean is at least seven miles deep, we can go down slowly. For, strangely enough, the ocean floor surrounding the continents slopes gently downward for some tens of miles before plunging to great depths. These gently sloping areas, the "shoulders" of the continents, are called the continental

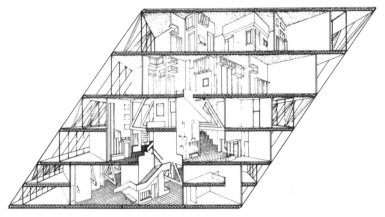

Cross-section through one wall of a City Shape/21 unit.

shelves. Geologically they are more similar to the continents than they are to the rest of the ocean floor. With an average width of some forty miles, and reaching down no more than about six hundred feet, the continental shelves cover an enormous area— some 12 million square miles. This is equivalent to discovering an additional continent larger than Africa.

The significance of this "find" can be appreciated when it is realized that most of the world's fishing grounds are located on the continental shelves, and that appreciable quantities of diamonds, coal, tin, gold, sulphur, natural gas, and oil are already being mined there.

Most of this has been done of course in the shallower portions. But increasing interest in the deeper sections of the shelves is being shown by government and industry alike. A wide variety of diving equipment has been built which will provide much needed experience in this strange, presently inhospitable world. Basically, all diving equipment falls into two classes: self-contained or scuba gear, and submersible enclosed vehicles that provide both protection and oxygen.

161

Normally, even if a diver carries his own oxygen down with him he can't descend too far because the ever increasing pressure acts on his body and drives gas into his tissues. At a certain point, oxygen becomes more poisonous than cyanide.

For deeper dives, the usual method used is the submersible, such as the submarine and bathysphere. In other words, the diver takes his environment down with him. While he is protected from the pressure, severe limits are set on what the investigator can do. Exploring the ocean depths from such an enclosure is somewhat similar to hunting frogs from inside your car. The ideal kind of exploration permits the investigator to swim around and make contact with his subject.

Even without such protection, however, fairly deep dives have been made. If the diver descends slowly his body has a chance to adjust to the differences in pressure and he can go down some hundreds of feet. The problem is the long period of time required for "compression" during the descent, and the even longer time required for decompression when the diver comes up. If this period is not long enough, the gases in his tissues expand and the diver is subjected to the "bends," which are terrible pains, and which eventually become lethal.

An interesting approach to living and working in the sea has now been taken, with Project Tektite 1 (see cutaway drawing). Here four scientific aquanauts remained for sixty days under forty-two feet of water. While neither the depth nor duration was great enough to break any records, the aquanauts were able to leave their "home" for up to five hours a day to perform experiments in geology, marine biology, and transmission of sound—all without having to undergo time-consuming compression and decompression. The secret lay on the fact that a hatch in the bottom of their home

Tektite I.

was left completely open. (No, water did not enter the vessel.
Insert an upended glass into a pot of water and see what
happens.) This meant that the pressure inside Tektite 1
matched that of the sea around it, and the aquanauts could
leave and enter at will. What happened was that the mixture
of gases the men were breathing entered (saturated) their
tissues and stayed there for the duration of the dive. Conse-
quently the technique is called "saturation diving."

Experiments are underway to provide the same capability
for depths down to six hundred feet, which means that practically all the continental shelves can be investigated in this
way.

Stranger yet are experiments which suggest the possibility
of obtaining oxygen directly from the water, much as fish do.
Perhaps we should remind you that certain sea dwellers, such
as whales and porpoises (both of which are mammals) must
come to the surface periodically to breathe. In the experiments under discussion here, it has already been shown that
mice, rabbits, and other small mammals are able to exist for

163

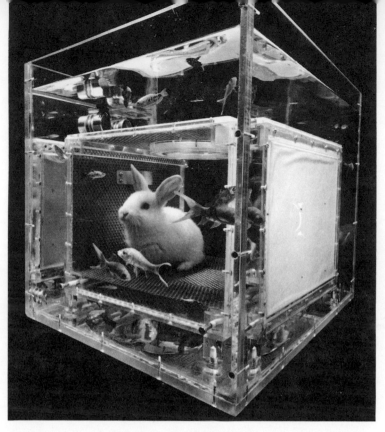

"Breathing" under water.

extended periods of time completely submerged!

Westinghouse is now building Deepstar 20,000, a manned submersible which will be capable of descending to and operating in depths of twenty thousand feet. This will make some 98 per cent of the ocean bottom available to scientific inquiry. However, the craft will have to be a stout one indeed to resist the incredible pressures of the ocean deeps. On the other hand, if man does learn to "breathe" underwater, the pressures lose their lethal quality; for his lungs will be filled with water anyway, thus equalizing the pressure inside and out.

164

Will this be the way people will live underwater in the world of the future? It could be. After all, man's evolutionary history does include a long period of time as a water animal. And developing human embryos still go through a gill period.

In the near future, however, we are more likely to see increasing use of closed craft, of larger and larger size. After an initial period of exploration, these will be supplanted or supplemented with permanent or semipermanent installations. The United States Commission on Marine Science, Engineering, and Resources has already proposed building laboratories on the continental shelf in areas of high mineral and biological concentrations. The Commission foresees these centers providing living and working space for up to 150 men. Contact with the upper world would be by radio, television, and mobile submersibles capable of locking onto and opening into the undersea laboratory.

There is no question in my mind that the next step would be undersea hotels, and then undersea cities. Perhaps they will at first be only the foundations for above-surface cities built in shallow areas of the continental shelf. But after that, completely submerged cities will surely come into being. Once again, says science writer Isaac Asimov, it will be possible to catch dinner in your front yard.

12

A Call To Action

UNTIL VERY RECENTLY, only a small percentage of the world's population resided in the forty or so large cities around the earth. But how much more than a small percentage of the world's medical treatment and knowledge came out of the large medical schools and hospitals and universities of those cities?

How many of the world's great artists, scientists, and musicians have come out of rural, backwoods areas, and how many from the great cities like London, Vienna, Paris, and New York? I'm sure you know the answer. Far, far more have come from, or at least were educated in, the large metropolitan centers than from small towns. Even Ben Franklin, this country's first scientist of note (among many of his other accomplishments), was a product, not of any frontier town, but of Boston, London, and Philadelphia.

It seems our frontier beginnings are so recent that we have not yet outgrown them. As a result we are living a myth. In spite of all evidence to the contrary, we still think of the independent, rural community as the backbone of the country. This is not true now, and it has not been true for a hundred years. The city is no longer the exception, and we must not go on thinking it is.

Max Ways, writing in *Fortune* magazine, points to two tremendous American efforts that were carried out more or less simultaneously in the nineteenth century: the conquest of the land by independent farmers and the assimilation (absorption) of great masses of immigrants from overseas.

The latter achievement was, in Mr. Ways's words, "at least equal to that of the pioneers who so fearlessly braved the poison-ivied woods across the Shenandoah."

Yet while the conquering of the frontier has been enshrined in American lore, the Americanization and urbanization of tens of millions of wretched immigrants is regarded as almost not fit for polite conversation.

But consider the significance of the inscription for the Statue of Liberty:

> Give me your tired, your poor,
> Your huddled masses yearning to breathe free,
> The wretched refuse of your teeming shore,
> Send these, the homeless, tempest-tossed, to me:
> I lift my lamp beside the golden door.
> *Emma Lazarus*

And they came, by the millions, when thrown out, misused, or ignored by the various countries of the world. And most of them came to the big cities of the United States.

Deplorable Conditions

European cities, over the centuries, have had a chance to adapt, to grow or shrink slowly according to need, and per-

167

haps to mellow as a good wine or cheese does. But the oldest
American city as such is only about 300 years old. Considering that a number of American cities are among the largest
in the world, we see that a period of explosive growth has
taken place. Indeed the growth of cities in the United States
over the past century and a half is almost without parallel
in the history of cities.

Is it any wonder that conditions in the cities have often
been deplorable?

Today the great torrent of immigrants from overseas has
slowed to a trickle. But now we find ourselves in the midst of
another kind of immigration—a movement from the rural
areas of our own land. Again, tens of millions of people—
for the most part poor, uneducated, untrained—have been
flooding the big cities.

Is it any wonder that conditions in the cities are often
deplorable?

We should point out, however, that there is a difference
between the two kinds of immigration. The difference has to
do with rising expectations, a term we used earlier. To understand this fully we must recall that all man's past societies have
been based on economics of scarcity. For a long time in man's
early history, simple survival was the prime objective.

With the development of agriculture a slightly more comfortable, though still marginal, existence became possible.
Even during the great ages of Greece and Rome and the
Italian Renaissance, relatively few people were well off; the
large majority of the populace was in rags, eking out a hand
to mouth existence. In 1854, almost a century after the beginning of Industrial Revolution, Thoreau could still write
that "the mass of men lead lives of quiet desperation."

168

In other words, the poor never expected to live anywhere but in hovels! It is only recently that they have come to expect more.

Yes, we still have the poor with us; but for the first time in the history of man it is widely believed that their lot *can* be changed, that everyone is entitled to medical care, an education, a job, perhaps even an income without a job, and a decent place to live.

The city is accused, abused, castigated—as if it were a living thing with a will, a desire, deliberately trying to hurt those poor souls who suffer in its midst. The city is blamed for the hunger, the poverty, the wretched living conditions.

But is it fair to blame a city for paying ten times more in welfare than a backwoods town in the South? Is it the city's fault that farm mechanization has thrown thousands upon thousands of unskilled workers out of their miserable jobs in cotton fields? Is it the city's fault that these people and their families have nowhere else to go *but* the city?

And why do they head directly for the great cities—New York, Chicago, Detroit? Is it perhaps because the smaller ones cannot handle them? Because the opportunities are even smaller in the smaller cities than they are in the large ones? Because these people are even less welcome in the small towns than in the large cities?

Those country (and city) folk who glower at the city should do the same at the safety valve on their steam radiator. For in truth that is what the city is. It gives the poor and the hungry and the strange a place to go—people who might otherwise make Home Town, U.S.A., a less livable place than it is today.

It also gives the budding genius a place to go—to learn, to

169

sharpen his skills, to earn, to make a name. Afterwards, when he can do so, he may leave the city—and then proceed to call it names.

A few will argue, not against cities per se, but against the immense size that some of them have reached. But here the problem may be that of an overemphasis on physical dimensions. The urban expert and sociologist Scott Greer suggests, "We must entertain the possibility that in social terms the contemporary metropolis may not be spreading as rapidly as we think. [For] when we remember the limits of communications and accessibility, it seems likely that [the Chicago of the horse-drawn street railway] was just as vast to its human population. It may be that the city is, in many ways, remaining constant or even shrinking because of the effects of instantaneous communications."

Along the same lines it is sometimes stated that the great size of cities like New York, and the even greater size of the metropolitan regions, makes the individual living there feel insignificant, that he can't "know" his city or region, and so on. Yet, does one feel less significant because he lives in a large and powerful country like the United States? Or does he perhaps feel a little bit *more* significant because of it.

As mentioned earlier, there are many levels of community —the family or home, the block, the neighborhood, the town or borough, the city, the region, the state, the country, and most recently (and for the first time), the entire earth. One can make, and many have made, significant relationships at each of these levels.

Travel times, for example, have been decreasing rapidly. On the national and international scale, travel times have been cut from months to hours. The future will see them cut even further, probably to minutes. The result, says Constantinos Doxiadis, will be Ecumenopolis, the universal city of man.

He feels that the continuous city is inevitable and will arrive no matter what is done to prevent it. Therefore, he suggests, our goal should be to divide or plan the city in cells, each one no more than a mile in length, and with cars relegated to tunnels and garages in the earth. Here modern man, like the ancient Greek, will be able to walk in peace and serenity.

Meanwhile, there are many more immediate problems. New York City, for instance, is said to contain fully half a million apartments in a state of decay, in addition to having a serious shortage of living space of any kind. In spite of massive expenditures and grandiose plans, all *cities* continue to fall behind in the task of providing adequate housing for their citizens. Again we take New York City as an example; at the same time that construction was started on 6,134 middle income housing units, an estimated 12,000 old buildings were abandoned by their owners.

Cities fall behind because of inevitable decay, because of massive inflows of people, because of tax inequities between city and suburb (cities have large welfare and education expenses which obviously should be shared not only by their suburbs but by the whole country), and because too many borough, ward or district administrations cannot get together. The New York metropolitan region has some 1,500 separate and distinct governments at various levels. The relatively small state of New Jersey has 567 municipalities, each with its own zoning ordinances and building codes. Since only one local government is involved in a city, it may prove

171

easier to rebuild city centers than some already deteriorating suburbs; it may even turn out to be easier than creating good, comprehensive plans outside the city center.

Another reason why cities fall behind is the population explosion. Wolf Schneider, in his excellent book *Babylon Is Everywhere,* points out that "In 1938 two countries, France and Austria, had more deaths than births; this situation no longer exists in any country on earth." Beginning after World War II the average yearly rate of increase of world population has been about 2 per cent. If this rate continues, in six hundred years we shall simply have standing room only— one square foot for each person on earth.

But long before then a couple with or without children would be lucky to have even a bedroom to themselves, let alone a whole house. Even in modern, industrial Tokyo the situation is moving in this direction. A vivid picture of what life could be like under such conditions is presented in "Billenium," a short story by J. G. Ballard.*

This is not the place to go into any more detail on the dangers of overpopulation, nor into what steps can be, have been, and must be taken to slow it down. We are, however, concerned with what can and must be done to accommodate those who have been brought into the world, as well as those who are housed unsatisfactorily at present.

There are a few, a very few, hopeful signs. One is the recognition, at long last, of the tremendous problems confronting us, and an apparent determination in some quarters to do something about it. The first agreements between a building trades union (the United Brotherhood of Carpenters

---

* In *Cities of Wonder,* a paperback collection of short stories edited by Damon Knight, Macfadden Books, 1967. This collection also contains E. M. Forster's "The Machine Stops," mentioned earlier.

and Joiners of America) and mass production housing manufacturers have recently been signed, indicating a softening of the building trade's traditional resistance to assembly line techniques.

Another small bit of evidence is an incredible outpouring of articles, books, and television programs on the subject. Dr. Glenn H. Beyer, Director of Cornell University's Center for Housing and Environmental Studies, points out that almost all the principal centers of higher education in the United States are now involved in top priority, future-oriented research into urban affairs.

Along with this we find increasing numbers of highly qualified professional people becoming interested in the problems —men like Air Force General Bernard A. Schriever (retired), who was a guiding force behind this country's missile program. (General Schriever noted recently that although he was supposed to be a technical expert he spent 75 per cent of his time getting people to cooperate!) He is now heading a group of men who, in cooperation with a number of private companies, are seeking ways to apply large-scale systems techniques to the problems of the cities. Several large aerospace companies are doing the same. And we have already mentioned the efforts of industrial giants like Westinghouse and General Electric.

In addition to books and people it will take money to do something about the cities, huge quantities of money. Some of the cost estimates are staggering. One—by the Swedish economist and sociologist Gunnar Myrdal—is that it will take a trillion dollars, and a generation just to rebuild and revive the big cities. *U.S. News and World Report* suggests a total of a trillion and a half dollars to create a model America.

It has been pointed out that in wartime we manage to find

173

the necessary money, no matter how high the amount. We are, the argument goes, in no less desperate times. We must therefore mobilize. The argument isn't a bad one.

Perhaps we shall have to pay more taxes. Well, so be it. Justice Oliver Wendell Holmes once said, "When I pay taxes, I buy civilization." In an interesting article called "Why I'd Rather Pay More Taxes," Professor Andrew Hacker of Cornell University points out that "Citizens of most other urbanized nations—for example, nonsocialist countries like Belgium, Switzerland and West Germany—pay appreciably higher taxes than we do. In return they receive substantially more civilization."

However, the economics of building and investment are complex and hard to fathom. Crawford Westbrook believes that there is money available to do almost anything, but that a major problem is getting those who have the money to work with the cities. He refers to cases where the big investors in a city have never met the city planners. In a number of European countries this is automatically taken care of by the fact that the national government is directly involved in the planning and direction. However, the idea of government control is enough to make the average American shiver.

But something has to give. Clearly conditions have reached a point where we must compromise with the situation. The President's Committee on Urban Housing, for example, recommends that the nation commit itself to producing at least 26 million new and rehabilitated housing units over the next ten years. This is an average of 2.6 million per year. Our present production is far below this—only 1.7 million per year.

The problem is that the cost of building has skyrocketed

and many builders no longer find it profitable to build housing for low and middle income groups. Almost 8 million American families—one in every eight—are not able to pay the market price for housing, at a rate that should be no more than 20 per cent of their total income. Dr. Doxiadis suggests a defense industry type of arrangement, in which the federal government takes over direction, while private enterprise does the work under contract.

Perhaps some of the experiments now in progress will produce a truly low cost building process; if so, the desperate needs of the country will provide the market. In the meantime, the federal government must step into the breach with tax incentives and rebates, low cost loans, larger grants to cities and states, support of research and development, and perhaps even direct building.

Unfortunately, even assuming the money can be raised, there is no agreement here as to just how to go about rebuilding the country. One urban planner pointed out that when John F. Kennedy decided a decade ago to build a moon vehicle, money was allocated and ten years was allowed to reach the goal. But, the planner added, at least we knew where the moon was.

The implication is that we don't yet know what kind of city to build, or what size, or how much public transportation to include, or how densely the city should be populated, and so on. There is not even a general concensus on whether there should be a national effort to build new cities and thin out the old.

In general, the solutions that have been proposed seem to reflect man's tendency to look at things in an oversimplified, "either/or" fashion. Just as literary characters are often

175

either good or bad instead of, as is usually the case, some mixture of the two, so too do city planners seem to fall into two classes—the city lovers and the city haters. The city haters, as we have seen, insist that the big cities are not viable entities and should be allowed to die, that efforts should be concentrated on rebuilding elsewhere.

The city lovers, who generally seem to be on the defensive in spite of the obvious trend in the direction of big cities, naturally support efforts made in the direction of perking up the cities.

Or perhaps the result will be a compromise. Perhaps we will countrify the city and citify the country.

My own feeling is that concentration along any of these lines, including that of compromise, would be a mistake. What should be obvious to all, but apparently is not, is that people are different—they have different needs, different desires, different tastes.

Yes, unplanned, disorderly growth is not good. But this does not mean that we should, as Frank Lloyd Wright suggested, abandon existing large cities in favor of Broadacre Cities (his proposal), or Radiant Cities (Le Corbusier) or Garden Cities (Ebenezer Howard). Of course, if we let things get bad enough, we may *have* to abandon our big cities.

Yes, let us build new cities, as many of them as are needed, rather than tacking bits and pieces onto existing ones. But let us not build them all to contain 30,000 inhabitants or 300,000 inhabitants, or 3,000,000 inhabitants. Let no one decide that this shall be the only kind available.

Whatever greatness there is in man derives from his incredible variety and diversity. How can he be expected to live in and be happy in one kind of place?

176

Brasilia, Senate and Congress buildings.

Somewhere, somehow, we shall have to learn the secret of the city, learn what to build into it so that we can build good big ones as well as good small ones. For building a big one that doesn't quite come off can be a very expensive failure. At the very least, it can only lead to the kind of cities many of ours are today.

We really have had very little experience in building new big cities. Brasília, the new capital of Brazil, is about the only one so far to reach any advanced stage of construction. About 300,000 people live there today. A dozen years ago it was a wilderness.

Hopefully, as we gain experience we shall do better in the future than we have been doing up to now.

The point is, assuming that a choice between large and small is provided for future generations, it should not be a choice between sparkling, new, well-planned small and medium cities, as opposed to dirty, old, and noisy large cities. Hopefully we shall have learned by that time how to make all our cities, even the very largest ones, beautiful and healthful, while at the same time keeping them, or at least some of them, full of spice and excitement.

A tall order, but one certainly worth striving for.

177

Bibliography

BOOKS

Abrams, Charles, *The City is the Frontier*, Harper & Row, 1965.

Advisory Commission on Intergovernmental Relations, *Urban & Rural America: Policies for Future Growth*, U.S. Government Printing Office, 1968.

Bailey, Anthony, *Through the Great City*, Macmillan, 1967.

Beckwith, B. P., *The Next 500 Years*, Exposition Press, 1967.

Blumenthal, Hans, *The Modern Metropolis. Its Origins, Growth, Characteristics and Planning*, MIT Press, 1967.

Collins, G. R. and C. Craseman, *Camillo Sitte and the Birth of Modern City Planning*, Random House, 1965.

Cook, Peter, *Architecture: Action and Plan*, Reinhold, 1967.

Dobbins, C. G., ed., *University, The City, and Urban Renewal*, American Council on Education, 1964.

Doxiadis, C. A., *Ekistics: An Introduction to the Science of Human Settlements*, Oxford, 1968.

——, *Urban Renewal and the Future of the American City*, Public Administration Service, 1966.

—— and T. B. Douglass, *New World of Urban Man*, United Church Press, 1965.

Ewald, W. R., Jr., ed., *Environment and Change, the Next Fifty Years*, Indiana University Press, 1968.

Faltermayer, E. K., *Redoing America: A Nationwide Report on How to Make Our Cities and Suburbs Livable*, Harper & Row, 1968.

Fiser, W. S., *Mastery of the Metropolis*, Prentice-Hall, 1962.

Fisher, R. M., ed., *The Metropolis in Modern Life*, Doubleday, 1955.

Fortune Magazine (editors), *Exploding Metropolis*, Doubleday, 1958.

Frieden, B. J., *Future of Old Neighborhoods*, MIT Press, 1964.

Futterman, R. A., *Future of Our Cities*, Doubleday, 1961.

Gans, H. J., *People and Plans: Essays on Urban Problems and Solutions*, Basic Books, 1968.

Genest, B., et. al., *Project Romulus: An Adaptable High-Density Urban Prototype*, MIT Press, 1968.

Gibberd, Frederick, *Town Design* (fifth edition), Praeger, 1967.

Gordon, Mitchell, *Sick Cities*, Penguin, 1964.

Gottman, Jean, *Megalopolis*, Twentieth Century, 1961.

Greer, Scott, *The Emerging City, Myth and Reality*, Free Press, 1962.

Gutkind, B. A., *Twilight of Cities*, Free Press, 1962.

Halacy, D. S., Jr., *Century 21: Your Life in the Year 2001 and Beyond*, McCrae Smith, 1968.

Hall, H. T., *The Hidden Dimension*, Doubleday, 1966.

Hall, Peter, *The World Cities*, Mc-Graw-Hill, 1966.

Hirsch, S. C., *Cities Are People*, Viking, 1968.

Hodge, P. L., and P. M. Hauser, *The Challenge of America's Metropolitan Population Outlook— 1960 to 1985* (prepared for the National Commission on Urban Problems), U.S. Government Printing Office, 1968.

Howard, Ebenezer, *Garden Cities of Tomorrow*, MIT Press, 1965.

Jacobs, Jane, *The Death and Life of Great American Cities*, Random House, 1961.

——, *The Economy of Cities*, Random House, 1969.

Jeanneret-Gris, C. E. (Le Corbusier), *The Radiant City*, Orion Press, 1967 (English translation of 1933 French edition).

Kristof, F. S., *Urban Housing Needs Through the 1980's* (prepared for the National Commission on Urban Problems), U.S. Government Printing Office, 1968.

Kulski, J. E., *Land of Urban Promise; Continuing the Great Tradition. A search for Significant Urban Space in the Urbanized Northeast*, University of Notre Dame Press, 1967.

Le Corbusier (see C. E. Jeanneret-Gris).

Liston, R. A., *Downtown*, Delacorte Press, 1968.

Lubove, Roy, *The Urban Community. Housing and Planning in the Progressive Era*, Prentice-Hall, 1967.

Mayer, A., *The Urgent Future: People, Housing, City, Region*, McGraw-Hill, 1967.

M.I.T. Students, *Project Romulus. An Adaptable High-Density Urban Prototype*, MIT Press, 1968.

Morris, James, *Cities*, Harcourt, Brace & World, 1964.

Mumford, Lewis, *The City in History, Its Origins, Its Transformations, and Its Prospects*, Harcourt, Brace & World, 1961.

——, *The Highway and the City*, New American Library, 1964.

——, *The Urban Prospect*, Harcourt, Brace & World, 1968.

Munzer, M. E., *Planning Our Town. An Introduction to City and Regional Planning*, Knopf, 1964.

National Commission on Urban Problems, *Building the American City*, U.S. Government Printing Office, 1969.

Osborn, F. and A. Whittick, *The New Towns: The Answer to Megalopolis*, McGraw-Hill, 1963.

Regional Plan Association, *The Second Regional Plan, A Draft for Discussion*, Regional Plan Association, Inc., N.Y., 1968.

Rodwin, Lloyd, ed., *The Future Metropolis*, Braziller, 1961.

Saarinen, Eliel, *The City: Its Growth, Its Decay, Its Future*, MIT, 1965, (original edition Reinhold 1943).

Schneider, Wolf, *Babylon Is Everywhere: the City as Man's Fate*, McGraw-Hill, 1963 (original German edition 1960).

Stein, C. S., *Toward New Towns for America*, MIT Press, 1966.

Steiner, O. H., *Downtown, U.S.A.*, Oceans, 1964.

Still, Henry, *Man: the Next 30 Years*, Hawthorn, 1968.

Tietze, F. J. and J. E. McKeown, eds., *The Changing Metropolis*, Houghton Mifflin, 1964.

Von Eckhardt, Wolf, *Challenge of the Metropolis*, Macmillan, 1964.

——, *A Place to Live: the Crisis of the Cities*. Delacorte, 1967.

179

Wall Street Journal (staff), *Here Comes Tomorrow,* Dow Jones Books, 1966, 67.

Warner, S. B., ed., *Planning for a Nation of Cities,* MIT Press, 1967.

Weaver, R. C., *Urban Complex: Essays on Urban Life and Human Values,* Doubleday, 1964.

Webber, Melvin, ed., *Explorations into Urban Structure,* University of Pennsylvania Press, 1963.

White, M. and L., *The Intellectual versus the City,* Harvard University Press, 1962.

Whyte, W. H., *The Last Landscape,* Doubleday, 1968.

Wingo, Lowdon, Jr., ed., *Cities and Space; the Future Use of Urban Land,* Johns Hopkins Press, 1963.

Wright, F. L., *The Living City,* Horizon Press, 1958.

ARTICLES

AIA Journal, "Anatomy of the Mall," February 1969.

Blumenfeld, Hans, "The Modern Metropolis," *Scientific American,* September 1965.

Boehm, G. A., "The Ideal City— Can We Build It?" *Think* (IBM), January/February 1968.

Business Week, "Master Plan for Revitalizing Fort Worth's Central Core," March 17, 1956.

——, " 'Metro' Has Another Fling" (re metropolitan government for Jacksonville, Florida and surrounding Dade County), March 29, 1969.

——, "A New Greek Oracle of Urban Planning" (C. A. Doxiadis), July 15, 1967.

——, "Prefab Housing Looks for a Home in the U.S." March 1, 1969.

——, "Railroads Spur Urban Renewal," April 12, 1969.

Cusack, M., "Are Our Cities Doomed?" *Science World,* February 29, 1968.

Carroll, J. D., "Science and the City: the Question of Authority," *Science,* February 28, 1969.

Craigie, Jill, "People versus Planners," *Technion Magazine* (Israel), February 1969.

Daedalus, "The Conscience of the City" (special issue), Fall 1968.

——, "The Future Metropolis," (special issue), Winter 1961.

Doxiadis, C. A., "Man and the Space Around Him," *Saturday Review,* December 14, 1968.

——, "Man's Movement and His City," *Science,* October 18, 1968.

Eberhard, J. P., "Technology for the City," *International Science & Technology,* September 1966.

EEI Bulletin, "The Year 2000" (special issue), October 1967 (Edison Electric Institute).

Engineering News-Record, "Fresno Mall Gives a Small City New Heart," January 12, 1967.

Esquire, "How to Save Our Cities," June 1968.

Feiss, Carl, "Taking Stock: A Resumé of Planning Accomplishments in the United States," in *Environment and Change: the Next Fifty Years,* W. R. Ewald, Jr., ed., Indiana University Press, 1968.

Fisher, John, "The Minnesota Experiment: How to Make a Big City Fit to Live In," *Harper's,* April 1969.

Freese, A. S., "The Crazy Things They'll Use to Build Your New House," *Science Digest,* February 1969.

Fuller, R. B., "Why Not Roofs Over Our Cities?" *Think,* January/February 1968.

Gould, Joan, "An Aquarium for People," *Esquire,* July 1966.

Graubard, S. R., "University Cities in the Year 2000," *Daedalus*, Summer 1967.

Hacker, Andrew, "Why I'd Rather Pay More Taxes," *Think*, January/February 1969.

Jacobs, David, "An Expo Named Buckminster Fuller," *The New York Times Magazine*, April 23, 1967.

James, J. R. and A. Derbyshire, "Planning for the 1970's," *RIBA Journal*, October 1967.

de Jouvenal, Bertrand, "Utopia for Practical Purposes," *Daedalus*, Spring 1965.

Lessing, Lawrence, "Systems Engineering Invades the City," *Fortune*, January 1968.

Life, "The U.S. City" (special issue), December 24, 1965.

Lowenthal, David, "Daniel Boone Is Dead" (re environmental pollution), *Natural History*, August/September 1968.

Lynch, Kevin, "The Possible City," *The Futurist*, October 1968.

McBroom, Patricia, "A Greek Vision of Tomorrow" (re C. A. Doxiadis), *Science News*, December 17, 1966.

McQuade, W., "The High Rising Monotony of World Housing," *Fortune*, July 1968.

Michaelis, Michael, "Can We Build the World We Want?" *Bulletin of the Atomic Scientists*, January 1968.

Mumford, Lewis, "Utopia, the City and the Machine," *Daedalus*, Spring 1965.

Nation's Business, "Rise of the New Cities," August 1968.

Perloff, H. S., "Modernizing Urban Development," *Daedalus*, Summer 1967.

Schubert, A. E., "What Nuclear Power Will Do to and for the Urban Environment," *The American City*, December 1968.

Science Digest, "City Planning Today," January 1967.

Scientific American, "Cities" (special issue), September 1965.

Siegel, S. N., "Electronics and the Urban Crisis," *IEEE Spectrum*, May 1968.

Spilhaus, Athelstan, "The Experimental City," *Daedalus*, Fall 1967.

——, "The Experimental City," *Science*, February 16, 1968.

Temko, Allan, "Which Guide to the Promised Land: Fuller or Mumford?" *Horizon*, Summer 1968.

Toynbee, A. J., "The Coming of the Worldwide City," *Think*, July/August 1968.

U.S. News & World Report, "Can Today's Big Cities Survive?" November 6, 1967.

——, "Cost of a Model America," November 11, 1968.

——, "How Building Costs Can Be Cut," January 20, 1969.

——, "Is the Big-City Problem Hopeless?" June 24, 1968.

——, "Latest Ideas on How to Save the Big Cities," February 27, 1967.

——, "A Look at Europe's New Towns," October 21, 1968.

——, "New 'Super' High School—Wave of the Future for Big Cities?" July 10, 1967.

——, "One Mayor's Story of the Mess in Cities," April 21, 1969.

Van Deventer, J., "Releasing Low Cost Building Technology," *Science News*, October 12, 1968.

Welsh, J., "New Towns: Made to Order, But Do They Fit?" *Think*, March/April 1968.

Wolf, Peter, "The Structure of Motion in the City," *Art In America*, January/February 1969.

INDEX

Advisory Commission on Intergovernmental Relations, 101
Air pollution, 55, 132-33
Air rights, 68, 145
Airplane travel; airports, 57, 58-60, 135
Algiers, 142-44
American Inst. of Architects (AIA), 67
American Institute of Planners, 84
American Society of Planning Officials, 84
Apartments, 35, 38-43, 47-48, 75-77 (*See also* Housing; specific locations); in megastructures, 136-37ff.
Aquanauts, 162-63
Arboretum, defined, 129n
Architects, 84. *See also* Building and construction; Planning, city; etc.
Asimov, Isaac, 165
Astor Hotel (NYC), 80
Astrodome (Houston), 52
Atchison, Kansas, 64
Athens, Greece, 61, 68
Augsburg, Germany, 82
Austria, 172
Automation, 110-11
Automobiles, 11, 61-62ff., 99, 100. *See also* Parking lots

Babylon Is Everywhere, 172
Ballard, J. G., 172
Balloon shelters, 28-30
Berkner, Dr. Lloyd V., 112, 113
Berne, Switzerland, 82
Beyer, Dr. Glenn H., 173
Bibliography, 179-81
"Billenium," 172
Birmingham, England, 98
Bloomingdale, Alfred, 151
Blumenfeld, Hans, 105
Bomb shelters, 70
Borie, Henri Jules, 136-37
Boston, 4, 13, 65-66, 75, 114
Brasilia, 177
Breathing, underwater, 163-65

Bridges, 19, 30, 68
Building and construction (*See also* Housing; Money; New towns and cities; Planning, city): city goes indoors, 49-60; megastructures, 136-47; new techniques, 17-33; rebuilding city center, 61-78; trade agreements, 173
Burbank, Calif., 64

Cables, cities hung by, 30-31
California (*See also* specific cities): new towns, 105, 106
California, University of, 106
California City, California, 106
Cars (*See also* Automobiles): electric, 65
Cellular concrete, 27
CERN, 131
Cherenkov, V., 60
Chicago, 67, 117-18, 141, 149
Cities of Wonder, 172n
City centers (*See also* Downtown areas; New towns and cities; specific places): planning for, 79-94; rebuilding and redevelopment of, 61-78, 107-8, 171-72
"City of Force, The," 33
City 1 (game), 91
Climatron, the, 54
Closet space, 48
CLUG, 91-92
Cluster housing, 37
Columbia, Maryland, 104-5, 127, 128
Columbia University, 93
Commuting, 98-100
Composites, 31
Computers, 88-91
Concrete, 24ff., 42
Connecticut General Life Insurance Company, 104
Conservation, 129
Continental shelves, 160-65
Contini, Edgardo, 141
Conurbation, 13n
Copenhagen, Denmark, 72
Cornell Land Use Game, 91-92
Craigie, Jill, 42

182

PICTURE CREDITS

Page

11 Florida State Road Department
21 San-Vel Concrete Corporation
22 Ewing Galloway
23 Hilton Hotels Corporation
25 Michigan State University News Bureau
26 Sikorsky Aircraft
27 Futuro Corporation
29 Goodyear Aerospace Corporation
31 Photograph by Ferdinand Boesch. Courtesy American Crafts Council
32 *At Home With Tomorrow* by Carl Koch with Andy Lewis, Holt Rinehart & Winston
37 Deeter-Ritchey-Sippel, Architects— Alcoa Properties, Inc., Owner
39 Glaverbel
43 Central Mortgage & Housing Corporation, Montreal
44 Swedish Information Service
46 National Homes Corporation
47 Owens-Corning Fiberglas Corporation
51 Westinghouse Electric Corporation
53 Robert E. Dick Studio
55 The Chamber of Commerce of Metropolitan St. Louis
66 Victor Gruen Associates
69 The Port of New York Authority
70 Alcoa. Photo by Bill Schropp
74 Westinghouse Electric Corporation
76 Metro Centre, Toronto
77 Metro Centre, Toronto
78 Seymour R. Joseph Architect. M. Paul Friedberg & Associates
83 Thomas Airviews
87 Life Magazine. Photographer David Lees

Page

91 Systems Gaming Association
93 Arteaga Photos St. Louis, Mo.
99 Flygfotograf E. Claesson, S:t Eriksg 24, Stockholm
103 Blue Ridge Aerial Surveys
107 Westinghouse Electric Corporation
115 Peter Wolf
117 Skidmore, Owings & Merrill Architects. Photo by Ezra Stoller Associates
124 Walt Disney Productions, Copyright, 1966
125 Walt Disney Productions, Copyright, 1966
127 Birdseye Aerial Photo
130-131 The New York Times
137 Peter Wolf
140 The Boeing Company
143 Ken Bell Photography
144 Daniel, Mann, Johnson & Mendenhall
145 *The Radiant City* by Le Corbusier, Orion Press
146 McMillan, Griffis, Mileto
147 Pilkington Brothers Limited, St. Helens, Lancashire
150 New York City Planning Commission
152 International Floatels
153 Pilkington Glass Age Development Committee
159 Reynolds Metal Company
161 Reynolds Metal Company
163 General Electric Company
164 General Electric Company
177 Pan American Airways